Multicultural Mentoring of the Gifted and Talented

Multicultural Mentoring of the Gifted and Talented

E. Paul Torrance
Kathy Goff
Neil B. Satterfield

Illustrations by Jamie McCracken,
Adapted by Ernie Hager

Prufrock Press
Waco, Texas
1998

Prufrock Press

PRUFROCK PRESS INC

P.O. Box 8813, Waco, TX 76714
(254) 756-3337 ▼ fax (254) 756-3339
http://www.prufrock.com

TABLE OF CONTENTS

ACKNOWLEDGMENTS

We are indebted to many people who contributed to the preparation of this book on mentoring. We are especially grateful to the following:

Chris Bennetts
Karen Bender
Dorothy Funk-Werblo
Krystal Goree
Frances Karnes and Tracy Riley
Marcella Kerlin
Jungjeun Lee
Jamie McCracken
Joan F. Smutny
All of the economically disadvantaged children
and youth whom we have mentored

E. Paul Torrance
Kathy Goff
Neil B. Satterfield

FOREWORD

In a manner typical of the master teacher and mentor he is, Paul Torrance, along with his co-authors, has made, with this book, not only a valuable contribution to the literature of mentoring, but also to the general field of creativity in education and, specifically, in the culture of poverty. This book has been under consideration for some time and is, therefore, long overdue but, as the reader is drawn into the world of mentoring and of creative education, he or she is also drawn into a review of some extremely relevant research in these fields.

As I became engrossed in this book, and I use the term engrossed in a most realistic way since the study and practice of mentoring are of primary interest to me, I realized that, for me, this story of mentoring was unfolding according to the blueprint of Torrance's *Incubation Model of Teaching*. The authors began by heightening my anticipation (Stage I) through a historical perspective. This included a review of Torrance's "Children's Manifesto," which has been widely disseminated, used extensively, and recognized as a credo for many in creative education. It has provided a valuable working guide for many children as well as mentors or would-be mentors from all cultures. Being included here, it becomes a credo in mentoring education as well.

The citing of case studies and personal examples took me into Stage II (deepening expectations) of Torrance's *Incubation Model of Teaching*, which I now experienced as a model for mentoring. My expectations were surely deepened as the authors expanded upon the elements of the Manifesto, using it as a backdrop to circumstances and activities in the lives of economically and socially deprived young people in the culture of poverty. I became especially impressed with the extreme need for mentorships in this group, where both the mentors and mentees have so much to gain ... or to lose.

In this extremely timely book, the authors have emphasized the need to appreciate diversity in order to recognize multiple talents in all youth. The dominant message is about creative positives, especially in the culture of poverty, with mentoring as the primary motivational intervention against the actions of gangs and the peer pressures of society. One of the cautions about pitfalls in mentoring is based upon the characteristics of the mentees in the culture of poverty.

Stage III of the (now) *Incubation Model of Teaching and Mentoring* (keeping it going) was exemplified in the inclusion of well-researched bases in mentoring, bringing together high-spots of other recent as well as earlier publications. I was reminded of some "tried and true" practices in mentoring, applied here especially to the culturally deprived. In adapting the *Incubation* model to mentoring as well as teaching, the authors discussed why and how it was suited to the strengths of the economically disadvantaged. Also, by concluding with the Children's Manifesto, the authors encouraged me to enter into the picture and become a part of the action.

Typical of Torrance is his unceasing crusade for all people to realize their potential, and especially through an emphasis upon their strengths. This book extends that crusade to include mentorship of the economically disadvantaged. Meaningful examples throughout the book as well as graphical illustrations of many of them enhance the message.

It has been very seldom, if ever, that I have been disappointed in the writings of Paul Torrance. He and his co-authors have, again, not disappointed me with this book. They have accepted the challenge of dealing with minority cultures, have taken that challenge beyond stereotypes, and have done it gently and in the spirit of "cheering one on."

Ruth B. Noller
Distinguished Service Professor, Emeritus
State University College, Buffalo

May 17, 1997

PREFACE

Each of the authors has had a long-time concern about the difficulties of the economically disadvantaged (people who live in poverty) and their lack of mentors. In Torrance's longitudinal studies of creative achievement, it was not even possible to locate most of the economically disadvantaged. Of the few we were able to locate and from whom we obtain follow-up data, not one ever had a mentor.

We recognized that there are many reasons for this state of affairs. The economically disadvantaged move frequently, become alienated from their families, are frequently homeless, engage in violence and other crimes, and the like. Their talent is often not recognized because they are poor.

In very recent years, there has been an enormous upsurge of interest in the promise of mentoring and efforts to initiate mentor programs. Schools, businesses, civic organizations, and governmental agencies have initiated mentoring programs. In response to this interest, many guides for mentors have been written. Our concern is that these guides fail to consider the needs of the economically disadvantaged and the problems that are of most concern to such groups. This contention is confirmed by Noller and Frey (1995, p.203), well-known authorities and bibliographers on mentoring.

It was for this reason the authors decided to join forces and write a guide addressing the real problems of mentoring the poor. When we finished the first draft, we recognized we were still not giving enough attention to the actual problems of mentoring the poor. We decided we would search in our own experiences to determine the differences in mentoring people who live in poverty and the more affluent whose problem we and other writers had addressed. Finally, we believe we have produced a guide that will be of help to mentors of all gifted and talented children and youth, with an emphasis on the problems faced in mentoring in the culture of poverty.

Of course, gifted and talented children and youth growing up in poverty frequently do not meet school systems' standards for classification as gifted or talented. However, if they are given encouragement, challenge, and caring guidance, they do attain these standards. Dorothy Sisk (1993) conducted a large-scale study in four locations, involving Hispanics, African Americans, and Navajos. At the beginning, not one of them met the requirements of their school system's gifted program. Furthermore, none of them was nominated by a teacher for such programs. After three years in a program that emphasized motivation, 50 percent of them met the qualifications for the gifted programs in their school systems. The same phenomenon is seen in mentoring programs.

Interest in mentoring needy children has been growing in recent years as a result of programs sponsored by various civic organizations such as the 100 Black Men's Clubs, Junior Achievement, the National Council for Negro Women, Big Sisters and Big Brothers clubs, tutorial programs, and the like. The movement was given a tremendous boost by the summit held in April 1997, and led by former Chairman of the Joint Chiefs of Staff Colin Powell, President William Clinton, and former presidents George Bush, Jimmy Carter, and Gerald Ford. The summit assembled corporate, political, and community leaders to make new commitments to the needy youth of our nation. Deliberate and vigorous attempts are being made to recruit mentors for this purpose.

Philosophy for Mentoring the Economically Disadvantaged

The authors believe that every child should have a fair chance to grow and to realize their potential. Of all groups, those who live in poverty experience the most severe obstacles to getting the kind of education that will give them the chance to develop their talents. When the economically disadvantaged are given such an opportunity, they are given all kinds of encouragement as long as they remain courteous, conforming, and accepting of mainstream values. If they fail to do this, they are ridiculed, rejected, excluded, and punished in an effort to reform them. Such children, however, are difficult to reform. Thus, they are likely to turn to delinquency, violence, and destruction or suffer from mental illness.

We believe that any system of education that aspires to give all children a chance to become whatever they are capable of must respect each child's individuality. We should stress the fact that recognition and acceptance of positive characteristics and strengths is necessary. A good mentor can do much to assure this.

We must accept the notion that people are born neither good nor evil but with innate potential for determining, in large part, their human development. We must reject the assumption that deficiencies motivate proper behavior and instead accept the more realistic belief that giving attention to successful behavior motivates the attainment of potential. This means recognizing, acknowledging, and using their potential to build success, skills, and abilities rather than wasting energy and resources by focusing on their deficits and neglecting their strengths.

We must reject the assumption that suffering builds character and instead encourage children and youth to cope constructively with predictable stresses and with the unexpected consequences of the risks they must take in attaining their potential.

We must reject the assumption that independence is the highest virtue and instead recognize that interdependence is the road to cultural competence and interpersonal satisfaction. This means the children will reach out into the community, the state, the nation, and to other countries, people, and institutions to get help and to give of their talents to their classmates, the school, the community, state, nation, and the world.

We must reject the belief that the only way a person can succeed is to best others and instead recognize that each person is unique and has particular strengths that must be valued.

We must reject the idea that there is a superior race, a superior sex, or a superior set of cultural characteristics and instead accept the fact that our strength is in our diversity. It means that we must recognize, acknowledge, and cultivate a variety of kinds of abilities or talents and achievements.

We must reject the assumption that the expression of feelings demonstrates weakness and instead accept the fact that the expression of feelings is essential to good mental health and to the realization of human potential.

It is also essential that we recognize the importance of the early years of a child's life and of teaching children almost from birth about their individuality. Education must become a continuous process in which both the children and society recognize, acknowledge, and accept their potential.

Programs for mentoring the economically disadvantaged must be open-ended but with enough structure to give guides for behavior. Mentors of the economically disadvantaged need to act as talent recognizers, acknowledgers, and developers. They must also give attention to the environmental features of homes, schools, and communities. Above all, they must attend to the strengths of the economically disadvantaged rather than focus on their deficits.

The Children's Manifesto

The Children's Manifesto, developed by Torrance, seems to summarize the things that mentors do to help their mentees realize their potentials. This manifesto may be stated as follows:

1. Don't be afraid to fall in love with something and pursue it with intensity.
2. Know, understand, take pride in, practice, develop, exploit, and enjoy your greatest strengths.
3. Learn to free yourself from the expectations of others and to walk away from the games they impose upon you. Free yourself to play your own game.
4. Find a great teacher or mentor who will help you.
5. Don't waste energy trying to be well-rounded.

6. Do what you love and can do well.
7. Learn the skills of interdependence.
8. Give freely from the infinity of your own creativity.

The authors have endeavored to give mentors the guidance they will need to accomplish this goal. We hope we have succeeded!

CHAPTER 1
MENTORING

Introduction

Numerous groups of educators now seem ready to do "something" about discovering and nurturing the abilities of students who live in poverty. Most groups, however, seem to be at a loss as to what to do. Many potentially positive contributions of hundreds of thousands of students from economically disadvantaged backgrounds have, for the most part, been lost.

There is a great deal of giftedness and creative potential among the economically disadvantaged. In longitudinal studies, children have been seen in the process of needlessly sacrificing what promised to be a great creative potential, and they may never regain the creativity they showed so abundantly in the third grade (Torrance, 1980). These children choose, instead, delinquency or crime or they suffer from mental illness—or, at best, a life of mediocrity, conformity, and unrealized possibilities.

Our educational system often penalizes children who are raised with different values and attitudes from those found in the dominant culture. There have always been many educators who believe that testing is an inappropriate way of evaluating human abilities, especially since intelligence tests have generally been designed for middle class, mainstream populations. Traditionally, extremely high value has been placed upon verbal skills, with the idea that if a person cannot express his or her thoughts then he or she is not thinking or is not capable of producing good ideas.

The truth is that we can be creative and productive in an infinite number of ways and that many important ideas are expressed in modalities other than words. In general, youngsters from disadvantaged backgrounds have lagged in their verbal development, especially in the kind of verbal development rewarded most highly by schools and tests of aptitude, achievement, and intelligence. Since people are motivated to do the things they do best, the overemphasis on verbal tests would not motivate a child who is behind in his or her verbal development to perform. Thus, it is practically impossible to determine the potential of a child or a young person who is not motivated to perform well on such indicators of ability.

However, there is considerable evidence to indicate that children who live in poverty perform as well on tests of creativity as more affluent students from the mainstream culture (Torrance, 1977). Many youngsters from economically disadvantaged or culturally diverse homes are capable of high levels of thought and learn well by experimentation, testing alternatives, and examining various possibilities. Lack of recognition and underestimation of the abilities of such children has contributed to the very limited successes of most economically disadvantaged children and youth in compensatory education.

Generally, programs for these children and youth have been based upon deficits and require that children ignore their strengths and work to develop some ability that may not be valued by their cultures. It is our contention that programs for the economically disadvantaged must be built upon the children's positives or strengths. The positives of economically disadvantaged groups include their creative abilities.

Members of these groups have had to maintain their creativity in order to adapt and survive. There is considerable evidence that successful programs for economically disadvantaged children and youth must be based on strengths rather than deficits (Torrance, 1977). Alternative programs for these young people must first find out what existing skills, abilities, and motivations the children possess and then provide for the expression, integration, and utilization of those skills.

Education is not limited to the classroom. Life itself is an education, and schools usually neglect the fundamental skills for successful living. Some of the key elements which are left out include:

- the purpose of life,
- the importance of forgiveness,
- the need for balance,
- how to figure out what we want,
- the usefulness of mistakes,
- how to love ourselves,
- the need for positive future images and dreams, and
- how to communicate with ourselves and others.

So what can be done to help these economically disadvantaged children and youth who have already fallen through the educational cracks and no longer attend school? This handbook targets those particular individuals, and we propose programs of mentor relationships.

What Is a Mentor?

The term "mentor" seems to have originated from Homer's epic, *The Odyssey*. Before Ulysses embarked on his 10-year adventure, he chose his wise and trusted friend (Mentor) to guard, guide, and teach his son. This model of mentorship has not changed much over time. Those who have guarded, guided, taught, and counseled young people in such relationships have varying labels in other cultures and periods of history. We have had "sponsor," "master," "tutor," "guru," "sensei," "patron," "coach," and so on.

The term "mentor" is the term which seems to have been generally accepted in the United States. Mentors are influential people who significantly help us reach our major life goals. They have the power to promote our welfare, training, learning, or careers.

Mentors are usually identified as having outstanding knowledge, skills, and expertise in a particular domain or area. There are additional characteristics of a mentor necessary to build a successful and creatively productive mentorship. One of the most important is sincere enthusiasm and caring. It is that experience of "taking someone under his or her wing." It is believing in the mentee's potential. (The word "mentee" will be used throughout this piece when referring to one who is under the protection or patronage of another.)

Closely associated to the caring

attitude and belief in potential is the ability to communicate clearly. This communication consists not only of content and processes, but also personal attitudes, values, and ethical standards. Positive, sensitive feedback regarding the mentee's development and progress toward desired levels of competence and desired behaviors are also essential parts of clear communication. A mentor sensitively listens to the mentee's ideas, doubts and concerns, despair and feelings of hopelessness, angry outbursts, and, sometimes, enthusiastic outbursts.

The mentor provides guidance to assist the mentee in developing to the greatest extent possible. Mentor relationships often require flexibility and a sense of humor to successfully negotiate problems which arise in developing such a relationship. Additional traits of a good mentor are:

- willingness to serve as a role model,
- willingness to give the time needed to develop the relationship,
- ability to praise and disagree whenever necessary and appropriate, and
- willingness to let go when the time comes and let the mentee fly on his or her own, but still being available.

The Importance of Mentoring

Mentors serve as wise and trusted counselors concerned with mental health, full mental functioning, educational achievement, and vocational success. Being a mentor frees us from establishing coercive norms and frees us to provide refuge for creative thinkers, especially when they are young. Mentors can provide children, adolescents, and adults with needed encouragement and a "safe" environment.

Torrance (1984) presents evidence that mentors clearly do make a difference. Men and women with mentors complete more education than those without mentors. It might be argued that the more education people acquire, the better the chances of finding mentors. However, only about one-third of the mentors were associated with college, university, or professional school experiences. Torrance

(1984) also reports that having a mentor is a statistically significant factor in adult creative achievement for both men and women. The presence or absence of a mentor makes a difference that cannot be explained by chance.

Mentors legitimize experiential and manipulative learning as well as learning by trial and error. Mentors encourage mentees to play with problems and dilemmas, look at possible solutions from various viewpoints, let one thing lead to another, and assist the mentee in creating visions and future images. What could be more important in today's ever-changing world than assisting creative individuals in realizing their potential and productively contributing to our society.

The findings and observations from Torrance's 22-year longitudinal study (1980) strongly suggest that the way to help economically disadvantaged children achieve their potential and to achieve creatively is through mentors. "Having a mentor" or "not having a mentor" had a significant effect on the children's creative achievements in later life.

Of all the economically disadvantaged groups the greatest concern has been expressed about Black boys. Their dropout rate and incidence of violence, robbery, rape, and other juvenile crimes are alarming. One organization that is successfully combatting this problem is the 100 Black Men's Club through its mentoring program for Black boys. One such mentor is Athens, GA's Charles Campbell (Morgan, 1995). Campbell is a deputy sheriff who spends most of his evenings and weekends in the community as a member of 100 Black Men of Athens and various civic organizations. He and all of the other members of this club mentor young Black boys who need such help.

Campbell is Hakeem Long's mentor, and he has now been in this role for four years. Campbell meets Hakeem at least once a week at Hakeem's school and at other times outside of school. At first, the other students thought that Hakeem was in trouble, because Campbell wore his sheriff's uniform. Campbell looks upon Long as his little brother. In this role, he doesn't have to correct Long like a parent would. Campbell said, "I just listen to him and try to be there for him."

Long said, "I used to get into a lot of trouble when I was in the sixth grade. … But now, I am a lot better." He has improved his academic performance and conduct. He was named the school's "Most Improved Student" during last year. Long says that it was because of Campbell that he was able to be better and said, "I'm sure I was headed for the Youth Detention Center if I hadn't met him."

There are many other stories around Athens about the mentors of the 100 Black Men's Club. The authors are impressed by the possibilities of this kind of mentoring. Another good example of the importance of mentoring is found in a report of a case in the Athens, Clarke County (Georgia) Mentor Program (Cox, May 13, 1996). The mentor is Judge Steve Jones and the mentee is a 10-year-old boy who has never known his father. Hoping to fire up his mentee's interest in politics, Jones and his mentee are working on a diagram of the federal, state, and local governments. In the process, the judge works in a few lessons about life in general. Although the mentee is only in the fourth grade, he says he wants to be a lawyer one day, and he has already spent some time in court observing his mentor.

The mentee said, "We have lots of fun, and we go to a lot of places. He's my friend, and he's like a father I never had." Judge Jones said he has seen the positive results that another supportive adult in a child's life can have. As a judge, he has seen some harsh results the lack of such a relationship can bring. He cites the time he had to sentence a 16-year-old to a lengthy prison sentence for robbery. Jones said, "I honestly think that if he had a mentor of some type that would not have happened. ... I think being a mentor is the most effective way to help kids. It's one-on-one."

There are many other similar examples of projects which are succeeding in helping economically disadvantaged children discover and develop their abilities. An example of one of these is an activity and mentoring program conducted by George Witt (1968) in New Haven, CT. At one point, he involved Yale students in a program in which each student was assigned to two children. The students helped the two children do their homework twice a week. It had been found that there was no place for these children to do their homework. Working with the parents of the children, volunteers built desks for the children to do their homework on. The students consulted with the children's teachers and involved the parents as much as possible. To help children who live in poverty it is usually necessary to provide such interventions to give real help.

CHAPTER 2
UNDERSTANDING
MENTOR RELATIONSHIPS

Mentors can be positive role models and can encourage their mentees when they are faced with alienation, exclusion, and disenfranchisement caused by societal stereotypes. Innovative mentor programs can provide children and youth with constructive alternatives to delinquent behavior if they instill pride in the mentee, aid in creating positive self-images, are prestigious or valued by their peers, provide adventure, and result in positive vocational strides.

Racial/Cultural Differences

Our society has never really dealt with racist practices which are roadblocks to the development of human potential. This has resulted in the proliferation of stereotypes or rigid preconceptions of individual members of particular groups along racial, religious, sexual, or cultural dimensions. Stereotypes are beliefs, acquired particularly in childhood, concerning characteristics of a group of people and applied to all members of that group without regard for individual differences. Stereotypes are the conventions people use for refusing to deal with each other on an individual basis.

Racial and cultural stereotypes can result in restrictive behavior in both minority and dominant groups. The self-fulfilling quality of stereotypes compounds problems as members of a stigmatized group often subscribe to stereotypic attitudes and beliefs about themselves. Consequently, many creative children of color, poverty, and culturally diverse backgrounds have severe problems in their search for identity and have tried to aid their search for identity and creative expressions through drugs, alcohol, or crime.

Atkinson, Morten, and Sue (1983) describe the five-stage Minority Identity Development Model. This model provides information on the stages and the changing attitudes during development. A brief description of the stages of this model include:

1. *Conformity stage*: an individual identifies more strongly with the dominant cultural values than his or her own, resulting in self-depreciating attitudes and beliefs; members of the dominant culture are admired, respected, emulated, and deemed superior; stereotypes are accepted and believed.

2. *Dissonance stage*: an individual experiences confusion and conflict about the values and beliefs of the dominant culture; he or she may actively question stereotypes, creating conflicts between self-depreciating and self-appreciating attitudes and beliefs; the individual experiences a growing awareness that not all cultural values of the dominant group are beneficial.

3. *Resistance and immersion stage*: an individual actively rejects the dominant culture and accepts his or her own cultural group's values, traditions, and customs; the desire to eliminate oppression of the individual's minority group becomes an important motivation; there is a feeling of distrust and dislike for all members of the dominant culture.

4. *Introspection stage*: an individual questions his or her rigid rejection of the dominant cultural values and the unequivocal acceptance of his or her minority culture; there is recognition that many elements of the dominant culture are highly functional and desirable, but there is confusion as to how to incorporate these elements into the minority culture; there is confusion regarding loyalty to the individual's cultural group and personal autonomy as the struggle for self-awareness continues.

5. *Synergetic articulation and awareness stage*: an individual selects elements from both the minority and dominant cultural values in developing a cultural identity; there is a strong commitment and desire to eliminate all forms of oppression; the individual develops a positive self-image and experiences a strong sense of self-worth and confi-

dence; the individual reaches out to different minority groups in order to understand his or her cultural values and ways of life.

Not only is it important to understand the developmental stages of minority cultures, it is also important to understand the developmental stages of the dominant culture in its awareness of other cultural values and beliefs. Sue and Sue (1990) have delineated the White Identity Development Model which also consists of five stages:

1. *Conformity stage*: an individual possesses minimal awareness of the self as a racial being, unquestioningly accepts the stereotypes of White superiority and minority inferiority and avoids any responsibility for racism.
2. *Dissonance stage*: an individual is forced to deal with the inconsistencies of stereotypes or encounters information or experiences at odds with compartmentalized beliefs; the individual may experience guilt, shame, or anger with the dominant culture's role in perpetuating racism or fear of speaking out now; there is a tendency to retreat into White culture.

3. *Resistance and immersion stage*: an individual begins to question and challenge his or her own racism; at first, racism is seen everywhere, and the person is likely to undergo a form of racial self-hatred; the individual reaches out but is often rejected.

4. *Introspective stage*: an individual expresses a greater need for autonomy and no longer denies that he or she is White; there is a reduction of defensiveness and guilt associated with being a member of the dominant culture.

5. *Integrative awareness stage*: a non-racist White identity begins to emerge; there is increased awareness of the sociopolitical influences affecting races and cultural relations, increased appreciation for cultural diversity, and an increased social commitment toward eradication of racism and oppression.

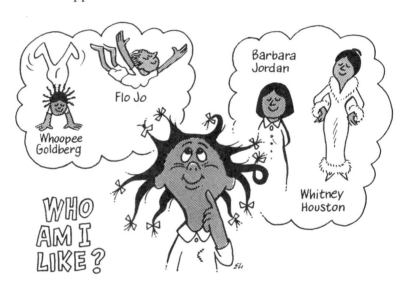

It is important for mentors who work with children and youth of different racial or cultural backgrounds to gain a better understanding of themselves as well as those they are helping. Mentors need to recognize that racial and ethnic backgrounds compound the problems of identity among the economically disadvantaged. They also need to recognize that the stages which Atkinson, Morten, and Sue (1983) described are never really clear cut with most people, but are fluctuating states of mind. People can embody several of them simultaneously depending upon the circumstances.

Characteristics of Economically Disadvantaged Children and Their Families

Using a variety of sources and drawing from our personal experiences, the authors have compiled lists of common characteristics of economically disadvantaged children and their families (Allen-Hagen, 1955; Close, 1990; Torrance, 1977; Witt, 1968, 1971). It should be recognized, of course, that none of these characteristics is common to every economically disadvantaged child. However, they appear frequently enough to be considered characteristic of them as a group. It should also pointed out that there is a list of negative characteristics and a list of positive characteristics, often referred by Torrance as creative positives. Economically disadvantaged children have experiences resulting from their poverty through which they develop these positive characteristics, as shown particularly by Close (1990), Torrance (1977), and Witt (1968).

Positive Characteristics of the Economically Disadvantaged
- Develop creativity.
- Are extraordinarily courageous.
- Overcome immense odds.
- Support one another.
- Are persistent.
- Are risk-taking and "gutsy."
- Have a charismatic smile.
- Have an extraordinary sense of humor and wit.
- Tend to see the bright side of any circumstance.
- Work to make others feel comfortable.
- Can "make do" with commonplace materials.
- Have ability to express true feeling and emotions.

- Enjoy story-telling, drama, and role playing.
- Enjoy drawing, painting, and sculpture.
- Enjoy singing, rhythm, and movement.
- Have expressive speech.
- Responsive to the concrete.
- Responsive to the kinesthetic.
- Are expressive in gestures and body language.
- Produce rich and colorful imagery in informal language.
- Are emotionally responsive.
- Are quick in warming-up.

Common Negative Characteristics
of the Economically Disadvantaged

- Exhibit disruptive and rebellious attitude.
- Are quiet and withdrawn.
- Have low level of self-esteem.
- Have lives that are complicated and out of control.
- Act quickly and impulsively.
- Have low tolerance for frustration.
- Feel that they do not belong in the school.
- Have poor social adjustment and skills.
- Are non-trusting.
- Feel that they cannot count on anything.
- Are unable to tolerate structured activities.

- Are often loners and not accepted by more advantaged peers.
- Have a home language or language other than mainstream English.
- Have low basic academic skills.
- Are bored with school and fail to see the relevance of education.
- Are more mobile than other children.
- Are masters of manipulation; are "con artists."
- Violate curfew and loiter.
- Have poor home–school communication.
- Are frequently absent or tardy at school.

Characteristics of Economically Disadvantaged Families

The following characteristics are found frequently enough to be considered common among economically disadvantaged families. Again, we must caution that not all poor families have all of these characteristics:

- Have many taboo subjects and many secrets.
- Have low tolerance for frustration and waiting.
- One or both parents are alcoholics.
- Are addicted to cocaine or other drugs and are dealers and pushers.
- Parents steal or borrow the meager earning of their children.
- Only certain feelings are okay.
- Have lots of shoulds and rules are inconsistent, unclear, and rigid.
- Atmosphere is usually tense.
- There is lots of anger and fear.
- Feel tired, hurt, and disappointed.
- Have feelings of low self-worth.
- Frequently have unmarried parents.
- Frequently have one-parent families.
- Have no sense of identity.
- May have sexually abusive parents.
- Frequently have poor communication among parents.
- May be rejected or for some other reason and have to live with grandparents, an uncle or an aunt, or some other relative or friend.

These characteristics may seem overwhelming to mentors but suggestions are given in later portions of this guidebook for dealing positively and creatively with them.

Cultivating a Mentor Relationship

Mentors for the economically disadvantaged will, most often, be working with a potential dropout or a child who has already dropped out in an effort to get the mentee's life—academically, socially, mentally, and physically—back on track. When a young person is paired with a mentor, he or she begins to evaluate the relationship either overtly or covertly. The mentor must be perceived as accepting, genuine, spontaneous, respecting, empathetic, open, and self-disclosing. May (1939) suggested four basic characteristics which are necessary for a mentor to possess in order to foster a successful relationship:

1) An understanding of personal prejudice,
2) A courageous acceptance of personal imperfection,
3) An enjoyment of the process of living—the means, not the end, and
4) A development of interest in people for their own sake.

One of the most beneficial characteristics of an effective, culturally flexible mentor is self-awareness. Additionally, the mentor must be committed, patient, willing to take risks, and willing to acquire a broad knowledge of human differences and similarities. A successful nontraditional mentor relationship is a creative experience since it must be open, flexible, and requires risk taking on the part of the mentor as well as the mentee. Therefore, we recommend focusing on the creative positives of the economically disadvantaged as the basis for cultivating a successful mentor relationship.

Creative Positives
of the Economically Disadvantaged

We are convinced that the positives of economically disadvantaged groups are their creative abilities. Members of these groups have had to maintain their creativity in order to adapt and survive. According to Torrance (1977):

> It is less condescending to recognize a person's strengths and to encourage their use in learning and in developing a career than it is to insist that a person ignore those strengths and work to develop some ability that may not be valued by that person's culture. (p. 23)

This belief led to his conceptualization of the creative positives after recognizing that the abilities and tasks that flourish in any culture are the ones that are encouraged or honored by that culture. Based on five years of work with economically disadvantaged children, Torrance (1977) identified the following creative positives of such children, characteristics that occur to a high degree and with high frequency among these children:

- ability to express feelings and emotions,
- ability to improvise with commonplace materials,

- articulateness in role playing and story telling,
- enjoyment of and ability in visual art—drawing, painting, and sculpture,
- enjoyment of and ability in creative movement, dance, and dramatics,
- enjoyment of and ability in music and rhythm,
- expressive speech,
- fluency and flexibility in nonverbal media,
- enjoyment of and skills in group activities and problem solving,
- responsiveness to the concrete,
- responsiveness to the kinesthetic,
- expressiveness of gestures and body language, and ability to interpret body language,
- humor and sense of humor,
- richness of imagery in informal language,
- originality of ideas in problem solving,
- problem centeredness or persistence in problem solving,

- emotional responsiveness, and
- quickness of warm-up.

Not all members of economically disadvantaged groups are gifted in all of these positives; however, these creative positives occur to a high degree among such groups in general. These creative positives can be observed among poor children by anyone who is willing to become a sensitive, open-minded human being in situations where trust and freedom are established. A brief description of each of the creative positives and some careers that seem to call for these positives appear below.

Ability to Express Feelings and Emotions

Middle class society has tended to belittle emotional expression, and education has stressed objectivity and suppression of emotional experiencing. It is obvious, however, that emotional expression is an important aspect of all kinds of creative performances in music, acting, writing, dance, and the visual arts. It is also clear that emotional expression is an important part of the ordinary functioning of a healthy, fully functioning human being.

Some examples of careers which seem to call for this kind of giftedness are: actor, artist, musician, dancer, composer, comedian, keynote speaker, poet, religious leader, salesperson, singer, and therapist.

Articulateness in Role Playing and Story Telling

Role playing and story telling are fundamental to the creative problem solving processes and achievements. Role playing and related techniques give rise to fresh ideas, different perspectives, and points of view while creating an environment for empathic expression between participants. Some of the numerous careers in which this talent is important include: playwright, inspirational speaker, story teller, novelist, comedian, politician, detective, actor, writer of children's books, historian, and religious leader.

Enjoyment of and Ability in Visual Arts

Many scholars in the field of creative achievement believe that visual artists have been and always will be the forerunners of human advancement. The visual mode of finding out and communicating is powerful and most people depend heavily on it.

It is difficult to think of a career that could not be enhanced by this talent. Some careers in which this giftedness is especially useful are: architect, cinematographer, photographer, graphic artist, fashion designer, jewelry designer/maker, sculptor, stage/set designer, art therapist, cartoonist, advertiser, and video artist.

Enjoyment of and Ability in Creative Movement and Dance

Middle class society has generally made this kind of performance taboo for its own members and only recently have educators begun to recognize the power of creative movement and dance as a medium for communication, self-expression, and learning.

While there are careers in creative movement and dance, there are many other careers that make use of this talent: professional athlete, choreographer, clown, dance therapist, recreation director, physical education teacher, gymnast, aerobic instructor, and mime.

Enjoyment of and Ability in Music and Rhythm

Music and rhythm are widely accepted as media of self-expression and communication and have been the bases for many highly successful careers among the culturally different. Music and rhythm are important tools for teaching problem solving, language skills, and other basic concepts.

Some of the more common careers in which this talent is important are: song writer, rapper, dancer, musician, sound engineer, choreographer, singer, conductor, composer, video producer, dance therapist, and music therapist.

Use of Expressive Speech

A number of linguists say that the standard English of mainstream society is overly vague and that much of it does not help express ideas. Many excellent ideas have perished and scientific breakthroughs have been lost because their originators lacked expressiveness of speech.

Expressive speech can enhance one's performance in almost any career. Some careers which are dependent on this type of giftedness are: politician, preacher, disc/video jockey, television interviewer, radio commentator, writer, teacher, rapper, entertainer, actor, story teller, lawyer, and salesperson.

Fluency and Flexibility in Nonverbal Media

Figural fluency and flexibility involve the ability to produce images. Some believe that this type of imagery is somehow involved in almost every kind of creative achievement.

Giftedness in figural fluency and flexibility appear to be far more important in many career fields than has generally been recognized. Some of the more obvious and common careers involving this talent are: illustrator, engineer, caterer, inventor, new product designer, humorist, improvisational actor, antiques/junk dealer, interior decorator, mechanic, photographer, tailor/seamstress, and pattern maker.

Enjoyment of and Skill in Group Problem Solving

In the early history of the U.S., great value was placed on the development of independent behavior. Schools have continued to encourage and give practice in such behavior, almost to the exclusion of cooperation and interdependent behavior. However, the complexity of life in today's society makes great demands upon skills of interdependent behaviors which has increased awareness of the need of developing skills in interdependence and collaboration.

Some examples of careers which rely especially on group skills include: construction supervisor, explorer, leader, military officer, space explorer/researcher, program director, consultant, coach, scientist, manager, union organizer, political campaign manager, negotiator, arbitrator, and fund raiser.

Responsiveness to the Concrete

While concrete thinking has been derogated as an inferior or immature stage of thinking, a large share of the world's most important work and achievement requires this type of thinking. This type of giftedness involves the use of hand tools and the physical manipulation of objects.

Examples of careers in which responsiveness to the concrete is an asset are: builder, construction worker, wood worker, engraver, florist, sculptor, mechanic, inventor, painter, technician, zoo keeper, photographer, set designer, magician, and plumber.

Responsiveness to the Kinesthetic

Responsiveness to the kinesthetic includes many kinds of skills and abilities such as psychomotor coordination, endurance, strength, flexibility in movement, and expressive/interpretive movement. A person performing purposeful movement is coordinating the cognitive, psychomotor, and affective domains. Thus, it is necessary to understand muscular, physiological, social, psychological, and neurological movement in order to recognize and effectively use movement potential.

Movement is an important key to effectiveness in all areas of life. The following careers are highly dependent upon this kind of giftedness: athlete, choreographer, clown, dancer, physical therapist, athletic coach, juggler, actor, acrobat, chiropractor, dance therapist, aerobics instructor, puppeteer, and magician.

Expressiveness of Gestures and Body Language

Expressiveness of gestures and body language as a creative positive overlaps somewhat with creative movement and responsiveness to the kinesthetic. However, its focus is on communication through gestures, body language, and interpreting this kind of communication. Communication through gestures and body language is an important aspect of personal functioning in everyday life. Accurately interpreting the communication of others through gestures and body language is important in all interpersonal relationships and thus is a learning process.

The following careers afford outlets for this type of giftedness: impersonator, clown, mime, nurse, doctor, psychologist, psychiatrist, salesperson, sports scout, teacher, counselor, entrepreneur, preacher, and orator.

Humor and Sense of Humor

Without humor, life would probably be unbearable to most people. Humor is a survival technique for many people, especially the poor. While humor, in some fields, seems to be taboo, giftedness in humor may enhance success in most careers. The following careers provide some of the best outlets: cartoonist, clown, comedian, entertainer, humorist, story teller, satirist, politician, writer, teacher, jester, animator, puppeteer, and keynote speaker.

Richness of Imagery

Richness of imagery has generally been viewed as a characteristic of creative products which may be visual, auditory, or kinesthetic. Creativity researchers have assigned roles of major importance to imagery in creative thinking, invention, creative problem solving and creative behavior.

Some of the more obvious careers involving the production of rich imagery include: video artist, actor, designer, inventor, story teller, song writer, playwright, novelist, artist, choreographer, make-up artist, costume designer, jazz musician, figure skater, poet, salesperson, lawyer, and architect.

Originality and Inventiveness

Almost all of the breakthroughs in science, medicine, art, literature, and education have come as a result of originality and inventiveness. In longitudinal studies of creative behavior (Torrance, 1980), measures of inventiveness and originality have yielded the best predictions of adult creative achievement.

Some of the careers which make heavy use of this type of giftedness are: detective, product developer, advertisement writer, toy maker, puzzle maker, mystery writer, legislator, script writer, short story writer, fashion designer, trouble shooter, cartoonist, comedian, consultant, and inventor.

Quickness of Warm-Up

At times, quickness of warm-up may be overrated, but there are times when it is essential to survival or successful adaptation to change. There are times when immediate response to problems is necessary and delays cannot be tolerated.

The following careers require quickness of warm-up for success: ambulance driver/attendant, athlete, police officer, comedian, lifeguard, physician, rescue worker, nurse, pinch hitter/runner, plant section leader, special education teacher, fire fighter, and trouble shooter.

Examples of people who came from the culture of poverty and used their originality and inventiveness to make breakthroughs as the results of mentoring are presented in Chapter 10.

Examples of How Economically Disadvantaged Children Manifest Strengths in Mentoring Programs

Examples of how the strengths of economically disadvantaged children emerged as a result of a mentoring and activities program conducted by George Witt (1968) in New Haven, CT. Some of them are described below:

Marsene moved from being a somber, over intellectualized weakling to having a vibrant enthusiasm, playful intelligence, high social control, and excellent mastery in swimming. His school work improved from C+ to B+ and he is a high performer in drama, music, and science. His writing has changed from prosaic essays to highly creative fantasies and poems.

Valarie is considered to be extremely gifted by her cello teacher. She has also shown much talent and progress in expressive writing and in art. She writes and draws most creatively about her intense musical involvement. She has been a B+ student.

Gerald has shown extremely high capacity for original thinking. His occasional vivid short stories and constructions have become more frequent. He is now working on sustained science projects. Gerald initially was without discipline and self-respect. Now he is much more confident and organized. He has also shown high dramatic ability.

Sharon has shown a high ability to formulate questions about her social and physical environment. Her intense cello involvement has decreased her tomboy behavior. She excels in chess and mathematics. In swimming, she has few equals.

Arthur has developed highly sophisticated leadership skills. He is an excellent swimmer and well on his way toward becoming a good acrobat. At the present time, he has tutoring four evenings a week since he decided to be "intelligent." His piano playing, acting, art, writing, and science achievements are all at least in the superior range.

Wayne initially drew stereotyped muscle men and did precious little else. He is now a superb artist and has become a B+ student. His reading, writing, and conversation suggest a shift from dull normal to superior mental functioning. His chess playing and violin playing are also outstanding.

John began as a quiet, somewhat surly, high strung child and has progressed to an ebullient and highly enthusiastic one. His writing is rapid and imaginative. He seems to be constantly writing book reports. John has shown a fine awareness of and ability to reflect the feelings of others. His artistic productions are vivid and, at times, rival those of Wayne.

These are just a few of the examples supplied by Witt, but these are enough to show what can happen in a mentoring and activity program such as this. These economically disadvantaged children would not have been able to manifest these strengths without the activity program along with mentoring. We cannot discover creative ability without motivation and the opportunity to practice.

Summary

These creative positives can be observed without the use of tests by engaging children and youth in challenging activities and can be observed frequently among economically disadvantaged children as well as more affluent ones. Our position is that with adequate and appropriate motivation, economically disadvantaged children will manifest as much gifted behavior as more affluent peers.

An example of this was observed in the last day of a three-week creativity workshop for disadvantaged children (Torrance, 1974). The workshop participants challenged the participants from the demonstration school for gifted children to a "brainstorming" contest. Ten four-person teams were selected from each group to participate in two rounds of 10-minute brainstorming sessions. The gifted children were all White and mostly from affluent homes. Thirteen of the disadvantaged children were Black and seven were White. The mean number of ideas produced by the teams of disadvantaged children was 202.4 with the gifted teams producing a mean number of 115.1. The differences between the means was significant at the .001 level ($t = 4.947$).

The creative positives appear most frequently when children are engaged in challenging and exciting learning experiences that give them a chance to use such abilities. The only kind of interventions which are likely to be successful are those that build upon the particular strengths of children—their creative positives.

CHAPTER 3
FACTORS INVOLVED
IN MENTORING

In this chapter, we describe some of the pitfalls to watch out for in the creation of successful mentor relationships. We hope that pointing these things out will help aid in their avoidance and alert the mentor to foreseeable obstacles.

Mentor Treatment of Mentee

A mentor encourages and supports the mentee in expressing and testing ideas and in thinking things through, regardless of the mentor's own views. The mentor protects the mentee from the reactions of his or her peers long enough for the mentee to try out some of his or her ideas and modify them. The mentor keeps the situation open enough so that originality can occur and persist.

Essential characteristics of a creative personality are a high degree of sensitivity, a capacity to be disturbed, and divergent thinking. Frequently, creative individuals are puzzled by their own behaviors and need help in understanding themselves, particularly their divergence. Mentors assist during these crucial times by providing understanding and helping the mentee cope with the crisis while also maintaining his or her creativity.

Frequently, the mentee's ideas are far ahead of his or her peers and he or she possesses an unusually strong urge to communicate his or her ideas and the results of testing those ideas. The mentor is a "sounding board" who genuinely respects the questions and ideas of the mentee. This support stimulates further explorations and imagination.

A mentor also supports a mentee by looking for opportunities for the mentee to grow and be rewarded for that growth. The mentor's networks provide him or her with information on certain opportunities such as scholarships, awards, grants, jobs, and special events.

It must be understood, however, that being aware of an opportunity does not guarantee the mentee success, for often the mentor lacks the power to deliver or the mentee may fail to meet the challenge.

Key Ingredients in Mentor Treatment
of an Economically Disadvantaged Mentee

- Be patient, be prepared to call on your inner strength and peace before starting with the disadvantaged. They will test you for your sincerity and commitment as soon as they believe you might be for real.
- Learn their name, "What they go by," "Where they stay" (not "Where's their home" or "Who are their family members" until you know them).
- Learn what turns them on recreationally, intellectually, and socially, and what their short-term goals are (often undefined). Long-term goals are almost always missing.
- Ask what he or she would like to be when he or she grows up, and discuss it. Ask them, "If you could be or do anything in the world, what would you be or what would you like to do?" This question usually reveals the somewhat futile view of what is possible for them in real life. At some point, this is a poignant topic for conversation.
- Help the mentee see that his or her status is unique in the

world, though it maybe not in his or her neighborhood, and help him or her feel special about it, not inferior or unwanted. Teach them to see that people who speak of or treat them badly are ignorant.

- Controls and rules should have a reason and in most cases should be acceptable to the mentee. Consequences of violating rules should be made clear and sanctions should be applied without prejudice. Even when rules are fair and clear, youth unused to rules being enforced, will test them and may think of them as controlling or threatening. In fact, abiding by them may cause a loss of esteem or status in the peer group who are not subject to the same rules.

- Give the child/youth some responsibility commensurate with what you believe he or she can handle. Acknowledge a good job and even a good effort when you believe the child or youth tried his or her best. Use partial success as a celebrative effort and help him or her learn how to do it better the next time.

- For the particularly troublesome child/youth, catch him or her doing something good and reward it instantly, even if it means catching the child not doing something bad. Define some behavior or lack of behavior as good, catch them at it, and reward them with a pat or a supportive word.

THAT'S THE WAY TO GO, IODINE! I'M PROUD OF YOUR ACHIEVEMENT!!

- Concrete rewards like candy, cookies, pizza, milk shakes, games, or material gifts are important symbols of caring. Be careful that they don't become objects for manipulation or favoritism (when more than one mentee is involved). We once thought these things were forms of bribery, but no longer. They should, however, become less important with time and the genuine affection of the relationship should gradually replace them. Words and deeds that build trust and the mentee's self-esteem become more important in the long run.

- In the cases of puzzling behavioral responses, wonder about the mentee's preceding behavior and probable feelings or motive for the response. If it still doesn't add up, sensitively explore what else is going on in his or her world. Chances are good that something is wrong at home, at school, or among the peer group.

- Whenever or wherever failure occurs or bad things happen, they should be analyzed both instrumentally and expressively, cognitively and affectively. Make advantage out of adversity.

- If the mentee's life experience has been filled with disappointment, and most have, don't expect trust to develop in a short time frame. Rule of thumb: For every year of life in a fractured, low income lifestyle expect at least a month of relationship with twice weekly contact before there is genuine trust. Example: It may take a year to win the trust of a 12-year-old when it comes to significant matters that require a major change in his or her lifestyle. It is still his or her decision.

- Roles and expectations should be clearly and sensitively defined, but not constraining. Structure and discipline should be provided for the economically disadvantaged youth. The caution here has to be awareness that by pubescence, many children who live in poverty have had little guidance or discipline at home. Therefore, a mentor or helper faces a tough transition which requires exciting activities, lots of personal attention, early success, and much encouragement. Eventually, patience and deliberation will become part of his or her repertoire.

- Physical violence is learned behavior. Prowess or success in fighting is an area of self-esteem because it represents one of the few areas where the youth has power and is recognized by his or her peers and has status. Therefore, a good fighter connects fighting with acceptance, and it becomes a major stimulus for continuing the pattern. If the violence is to end, it must be replaced with new arenas of success and expression.

- "Street savvy" such as stealing, selling drugs, or fooling authorities is another means of status and reward. Removal from the temptation or opportunity is, in most cases, unrealistic. Therefore, time away from the environment doing exciting, positive things holds promise. The mentor must give enough of his or her time with these things to make the negative opportunities minimal in order to neutralize them.
- Involve significant other, such as guardians, grandmothers, mothers, aunts, and especially male figures, if there are any, to be part of the support network.
- Allow yourself (mentor) to make mistakes, to be human and self-forgiving. Religious faith may help here. Use your failures, frustrations, and anger when things don't work out to become a medium for discussion and plans for revisions.
- The unconscious fear of losing the mentor poses problems in sharing deep emotions, but evasion of feelings is not growthful. Separation anxiety should be dealt with carefully. Review shared experiences—knowledge and feelings. Talk about what both the mentor and mentee can take with them to the next chapter of their lives. Recognize one another's importance to each other, realizing that the separation will be painful, joyful, and strengthening because you learned and shared together.

Obstacles to Mentor Relationships

Some of the barriers to mentor relationships were identified in the key ingredients above. This section will briefly hit upon some specific barriers to mentoring economically disadvantaged children/youth. Generally, such children, creative or not, are not provided with well-structured learning situations supervised by empathetic, attentive adults. Economically disadvantaged youth have precious few concrete learning experiences that go beyond demanding imitative or compliant responses.

It seems that parents living in squalor do not efficiently supervise their children's school-related activities. The children arrive at school irregularly, no books in hand, empty of breakfast, and empty of self-esteem. Parents just do not seem to be able to get their children to do their homework, and many scarcely communicate with their children about that "alien" school.

Disadvantaged families generally do not use the printed word. Children are not taught to read by the parents/guardians, since the parents/guardians generally read only a little or not at all. Adults speak sharply to the children to give orders. The child quickly learns to avoid talking with adults because it is associated with unpleasantness. Long stretches of verbal silence signify that everything is going all right.

Frequently, the heads of economically disadvantaged households, by virtue of their low skill level or job discrimination, relate to the outer world in positions of low status and as victims of circumstances. The tasks assigned to them are primarily nonverbal and they come home continuing this mode of relating. Often, they bring home anger and resentment which is not expressed in words but in actions.

The economically disadvantaged child/youth enters school with a motoric orientation, using a different language for different functions, and becomes very restless when required to sit still and attend to irrelevant, incomprehensible school demands. Lack of food, shelter, and income can create problems which do not ordinarily occur for a middle class child. Consequently, the need for mentors for this population is paramount.

In any human interaction, there are phases of growth and decline. Disillusionment can occur when either party fails to live up to expectations. Parting, inevitable and even agreed upon, can be painful, especially to the one left behind. There are barriers to mentor relationships. We will discuss some of the more frequently mentioned ones. We stand a better chance of avoiding some of these pitfalls if we are aware of what they might be.

In some cases, the mentor's pace is too fast or too slow for the mentee. If it is too slow, the mentee grows impatient and gradually moves away from the mentor. More frequently, however, the mentor's pace is too fast—the mentor is too ambitious or expects too much.

Some mentor relationships weaken and die when the mentee develops a growing suspicion about the sacrifices of personal integrity made by their mentors. Mentees also drift away from their mentors when they find the mentors too limited in perspective and unable to look beyond present trends.

Many mentor relationships deteriorate and die when the mentee engages in behavior not approved of by the mentor or behavior perceived by the mentee as being disapproved of by the mentor. This occurs when the mentee accepts values different from the mentor's or accepts standards below the mentor's expectations.

Mentor relationships seem to wither when the mentee does not earn a living in his or her favorite field. Many participants are so busy that they have difficulty maintaining mentor and other relationships once considered meaningful and precious.

Many mentors become frightened of the mentees' original ideas exactly when support is needed. Many creative young people find they have to develop their own jobs and careers. Strangely, the creation of an unconventional career seems to doom mentor relationships. It may have been that these mentor relationships had limited depth and caring.

Some young women seem to have experienced a lack of closeness in their male mentors and have searched in vain for female mentors. Frequently, young women's mentor relationships end when they leave their careers to start families.

The most frequently offered reason for terminating the mentor relationships is geographical distance. Of course, many mentorships survive considerable separation while others continue at great distances. Nevertheless, "moving away" and the consequent separation is the single most frequently mentioned reason for the death of mentor relationships.

Gender Differences

Historically, most mentors have been men partly because there are more men in positions to assume mentor roles. As more women move into executive positions and other leadership roles, there will be more women available to become mentors. Torrance (1984) reports that there are indications that the needs of men and women for a mentor differ in some ways.

Women with male mentors report a greater need for a more personal or friendship relationship than did their counterparts with female mentors (Torrance, 1984). Males more frequently prized the mentor's skill and expertise while females more frequently prized their mentor's encouragement and praise. Both sexes equally value the friendship of the mentor relationship. Males indicated that they need mentors who are active, challenging, committed and dedicated, controversial, courageous, guiding, hardworking, involved, in love with their work, motivated for excellence, problem solvers, receptive, and stern.

The characteristics of mentors which females indicated they need are the ability to acknowledge the talents of others, articulateness, calmness, consideration of alternatives, confidence giving, controlled, empathetic, enthusiastic, facilitative, even-tempered, humble, idealistic, patient, nonviolent in philosophy, relaxed, thorough, vital, and witty.

The characteristics which seemed to alienate women include ambitiousness, compulsivity to work, critical in judgment, dominating and intimidating manner, lack of empathy, lack of future orientation, hypocrisy, intolerance of the ideas of others, inflexibility, perfectionism, and trendiness.

Multicultural Awareness

All mentoring is, to some extent, multicultural. On the one hand, each mentor or mentee brings cultural influences into the mentor relationship. On the other hand, culture is within each person, combining many different social roles into his or her basic identity. Understanding group differences, as well as individual differences, is important for the accurate interpretation of behaviors.

Multicultural awareness provides the opportunities for understanding different perspectives within each of us. According to Pedersen (1988), "Developing multicultural awareness is not an end in itself, but rather a means toward increasing a person's power, energy, and freedom of choice in a multicultural world" (p. 3).

"Awareness," according to Pedersen (1988), "is the ability to accurately judge a cultural situation from both one's own and the other's cultural viewpoint" (p. 12). Pedersen cites the following characteristics of an individual who possesses such an awareness (p. 13):

- ability to recognize direct and indirect communication styles,
- sensitivity to nonverbal cues,
- awareness of cultural and linguistic differences,
- interest in the culture,
- sensitivity to the myths and stereotypes of the culture,
- concern for the welfare of persons from other cultures,
- ability to articulate elements of his or her own culture,
- appreciation for multicultural teaching, and
- accurate criteria for objectively judging "goodness" and "badness" in the other culture.

There are numerous techniques to stimulate multicultural aware-ness. Experiential exercises such as role playing, role reversal, and simulations are effective in gaining understandings of cultural diversity. Field trips, discussions, and bicultural experiences can also stimulate multicultural awareness. The following section will discuss some specific strategies and techniques which can be used in facilitating learning and tapping awareness.

CHAPTER 4
LEARNING STRATEGIES
FOR MENTORING

We believe that the creative abilities of the economically disadvantaged are their strengths as described in Chapter 2. So how can these strengths be encouraged and developed? This chapter provides a three-step model to follow in creating presentations or activities for a mentoring/learning process and techniques for encouraging participation and creative expression.

Facilitating Learning and Creativity

People prefer to learn creatively—by exploring, questioning, experimenting, manipulating, rearranging, testing and modifying, looking, feeling, and then thinking about it—incubating. Schools and traditional educational settings have insisted that people learn by authority, by being told, because it is more economical. However, Torrance (1970) has taken the controversial position that many things can be learned more economically and effectively if they are learned in creative ways rather than by authority. He maintains that some people have a strong preference for learning in more natural ways than by authority.

To learn creatively, a person must first become aware of gaps in knowledge, disharmonies, or problems calling for new solutions. This is followed by a search for information concerning the missing elements or difficulties, trying to identify the difficulty or gap in knowledge. Next, there is a search for solutions, making guesses or approximations, formulating hypotheses, thinking of possibilities, and predicting. Then comes the testing, modifying, retesting, and perfecting of hypotheses, ideas, or other creative products. This is followed by the important process of puzzling over it, mulling it over, fitting the pieces together—incubation. Finally, there is the communication of results, a natural process. Strong motivations are at work at each stage and once the process is set in motion, it is difficult to stop.

People are inquisitive, exploring, searching kinds of beings. We are self-acting and cannot keep our restless minds inactive even when there are no problems pressing for solution. We continue to find problems and cannot keep from digging into things, turning things over in our minds, trying out new combinations, searching for new relationships and struggling for new insights. Creative ways of learning develop the motivations and skills for lifelong learning.

Incubation Model of Teaching

Torrance (1979a; Torrance & Safter, 1990) has developed a three-stage teaching model, the *Incubation Model of Teaching*, which provides opportunities to incorporate creative thinking abilities into any topic or activity. In using the model, an activity consists of three stages:

    1) warm-up or heightening anticipation,
    2) deepening expectations or digging in, and
    3) going beyond or keeping it going.

The purpose of the first stage is to create the desire to know or learn, to arouse curiosity, to tickle the imagination, and to give purpose and motivation. The purpose of the second stage is to go beyond the surface or warm-up and to look deeper into the information. For creative thinking to occur, there must be ample opportunity for one thing to lead to another, which involves deferring judgment, making use of all of the senses, opening new doors, and targeting problems to be considered or solutions to try. The purpose of the third stage is to genuinely encourage creative thinking beyond the learning environment in order for new information or skills to be incorporated into daily lives.

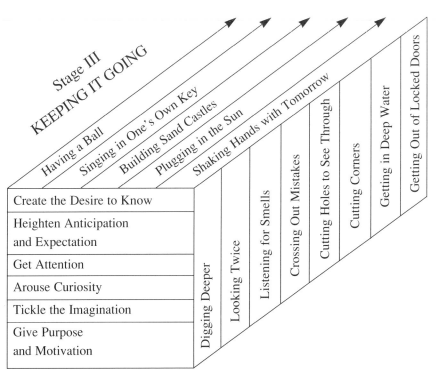

Figure 1. The Incubation Model of Teaching and Mentoring

There are many ways to warm-up to an activity. Some warm-ups include actual physical stretching and breathing to music in order to clear the cobwebs and get the blood circulating. Other warm-ups include visualizations to get the mentee thinking about the topic of the activity, imaging. Visualizations arouse the senses and get the mentee thinking about and being a part of the activity.

Warm-up might include things to touch or hear. Brainstorming is another good warm-up technique. For example, if the activity is on recycling, participants might be asked to brainstorm things that can be or are recycled, or brainstorm ways in which they do recycle, such as:

- using plastic berry baskets for strainers,
- covering old records with aluminum foil and using them as disposable cookie or cake platters,
- cutting plastic jugs to make scoops for dog food or potting soil.

The second stage involves looking more deeply into the activity. In a recycling activity, a swap box can be set up in a well-traveled area and used for the mentees to bring things which they do not recycle and swap them for items they can use. These items might include:

- buttons
- cards and calendars
- containers
- magazines
- oatmeal boxes

- pie tins
- rope and string
- shells
- wood scraps
- yarn

For this activity, the mentor can bring several of these recyclable items and have the mentees brainstorm uses for the items. Children who live in poverty are usually good at this kind of activity—innovatively using commonplace materials.

The third stage involves making the experience real. The third stage of the recycling lesson involves encouraging the mentees to bring items from home for the swap box. Garage sales are a fun way to turn lots of unwanted possessions into quick cash. A garage sale could be held to raise money for a camping trip. Another possibility is to set up recycling bins and organizing the distribution of the collected materials to raise money. The mentee makes a personal connection with the learning and gains relevant, real life experience.

This three-stage model can be used for any type of presentation or learning activity. Many times in learning situations, a teacher will warm the learner up and get his or her curiosity up and then proceed to give him or her the information. However, rarely is the information accompanied with an explanation of how it is beneficial to the child in his or her everyday life. As we stated earlier, many poor children do not see how the "foreign" mainstreamed information relates to their lives or how the information is beneficial to them. That is why the third stage is *so* important in the education of economically disadvantaged children and youth.

The *Incubation Model of Mentoring* is ideally suited to the strengths of the economically disadvantaged. They are curious and are quick to warm up. They want to know the purpose and are motivated by knowing the purpose. They are not satisfied by a superficial understanding. They love to dig deeper and look at their problems in different ways. They are willing to cross out their mistakes and find ways of "getting out of deep water." On their own, they enjoy playing around with what they have learned, talking about it and finding out more. They like to make what they have learned their own, applying it to themselves. They like to fantasize about ultimately doing something with it.

Brainstorming

One technique which can be used in all three stages is brainstorming. Brainstorming is a technique for strengthening the imagination and increasing flexible thinking and creativity. It is one of the most teachable procedures for deliberately increasing the number, originality, and quality of alternative ideas. It is a technique which can be used individually or in groups and provides opportunities to experience active learning while encouraging participation.

Brainstorming was introduced by Alex Osborn (1963) as an element of the creative problem solving method. Brainstorming skills can be developed when practiced with content or when practiced solely for skill development. It is an excellent technique for strengthening communication and discussion skills.

The heart of creative problem solving is the production of many alternatives, some of which go beyond the logical or rational. The technique of brainstorming not only improves ability to produce alternatives, but also to consider many alternatives. Four basic rules govern this process and success depends upon the degree to which you apply them. These rules are:

1) *Criticism is ruled out.* Do not criticize or evaluate any idea produced; record any and every idea. This is one of the most important rules and one of the most difficult to master.
2) *Freewheeling is welcomed.* The wilder the idea the better. Offbeat, impractical, silly ideas may trigger a practical breakthrough idea which might not otherwise occur.
3) *Quantity is desired.* The greater the number of ideas produced, the greater the likelihood of useful, original ideas. This includes bringing out those obvious, small ideas as well as the wild, unusual, clever ideas.
4) *Combination and improvement are sought.* Combine, hitchhike, improve, change ideas; new ideas lead to more new ideas. Group members are encouraged to hitchhike or think of ways in which the ideas of other members can be turned into better ideas, or how two or more ideas can be combined into a still better idea.

It is important to record and reward thereby every contribution—tape recorder, someone at a blackboard, or video camera. If the flow of ideas slows down or stops, the facilitator may ask questions to stimulate the flow, that is, What if it were much larger or smaller? What if it were a different color or multi-colored? What might be other uses?

The brainstorming technique used with groups gives mentees the opportunity to generate a multitude of ideas and at least one of them will be truly useful, innovative, and workable. Asking mentees for their input gives them an added sense of importance and creates an atmosphere for truly creative and imaginative ideas to surface and be acknowledged.

Brainstorming can be used anytime there is a gap in information, a problem, or question. It is a technique that can be used individually or in groups. Brainstorming stimulates and generates enthusiasm as well as promoting spontaneity and creativity. Mentees develop an awareness of seeing things from different points of view and experience a supportive environment for their creative expressions.

Provocative Questioning

Almost every mentor could improve creativity immediately by asking more provocative questions. Doing this makes learning more exciting and increases the acquisition of information, improves the ability to recall information in problem solving, and provides a more in depth understanding.

As a result of formal schooling, mentees often suppose that any question has a single correct answer. Thus, they need to be encouraged to think divergently. Types of divergent thinking are:

- *Fluency*, production of as many ideas as possible, emphasis is on quantity.
- *Flexibility*, shifting to a variety of approaches or ways of looking at things.
- *Originality*, unusual or uncommon ideas, ideas no one else will think of.
- *Elaboration*, working out the details of an idea.

Osborn (1963) and Parnes (1967) recommended the following set of questions to motivate divergent kinds of thinking:

WHAT IS IT THAT CAN MAKE THESE COOKIES ORIGINAL...EXOTIC... YET EDIBLE ?

Hmm...Think I'll nap on it for a while...

NEEDS CATMINT SLURRY!

- What would happen if we made it larger? Smaller?
- What could we add? Substitute?
- What would happen if we took it apart? Rearranged it?

- What would happen if we multiplied it? Changed its position?
- What would happen if we gave it motion? Odor? Light? Sound? Different color?
- What would happen if we changed its shape? Made it stronger? Put it to other uses? Made it of different materials?

Role Playing

We usually think of role playing as a group method, but it can also be a powerful tool in a one-on-one relationship such as mentoring or tutoring. Lawyers use it in rehearsing clients for a forthcoming interview. Mentors can use it to rehearse a mentee for an employment interview; a feared encounter; a peace-making confrontation with a parent, teacher, or friend who has been offended; and even to say "no" to pressures to do wrong. The mentee plays himself and the mentor plays the teacher, friend, parent, employer, or the like. Or, they might reverse roles, if the mentee is having difficulty in seeing the problem from the teacher's or parent's point of view. By doing these things, the mentee can overcome his fears about an encounter and think the problem through in a safe situation with the mentor.

Torrance has co-authored a book on *Creative Problem Solving through Role Playing* (Torrance, Murdock, & Fletcher, 1996) which describes several production techniques which are useful in a mentoring situation. Besides the role reversal techniques described above, there are the soliloquy, magic shop, mirror, and futures projection techniques.

.

CHAPTER 5
POSITIVES OF MENTORING

Maintaining a positive attitude in mentoring relationships is of paramount importance. By positive attitude, we do not mean an overly permissive attitude or a "yes man." We mean an optimistic outlook toward the mentee and his or her ideas or products. This chapter includes tips for providing positive feedback, a discussion of the benefits of a mentor/mentee relationships and aspects of a successful mentor relationship.

Providing Feedback and Support

A mentor provides understanding as well as giving guidance and encouragement. A mentor must be able to communicate sensitive feedback regarding the mentee's products as well as a caring attitude and belief in the mentee's potential. Flexibility and a sense of humor are important qualities when providing comments and suggestions to the mentee. Providing positive feedback without giving offense or arousing resentment is extremely important when dealing with a vulnerable mentee. Some tips are:

- Begin with praise and honest appreciation. (See Appendix A for 99 ways of saying "very good.")
- Call attention to mentee's mistakes indirectly.
- Talk about your own mistakes before criticizing others.
- Ask questions instead of giving direct orders.
- Let the other person save face.
- Praise the slightest improvement and praise every improvement. Be hearty in your commendation and lavish in your praise.

Anyone who wants to improve relationships with others needs only show a sympathetic understanding. Look for something in another person which you admire and tell him or her about it. All of us need to feel needed and admired. Encouragement through

47

praise is the most effective method of getting people to do their best. Adding to their self-esteem makes people want to like you and to cooperate with you.

Benefits to Mentees

Throughout this work, we have been discussing the characteristics of mentors. According to Collins (1983), a mentor:

1) gives upward mobility to career,
2) boosts self-esteem by believing in the mentee,
3) shares the mentee's dream,
4) gives vision by sharing dreams, goals, and insights into life with the mentee,
5) provides advice, counsel, and support,
6) teaches by example,
7) imparts valuable "inside" information (short cuts or information not readily available),
8) gives feedback about mentee's progress, and
9) cheers the mentee on.

Mentors provide protégés with support, encouragement, know-how, and skills. Bova and Phillips (1984) have outlined general skills that mentees learn:

1) risk-taking skills,
2) communication skills—listening, sharing,
3) political skills of the organization/school,
4) specific skills—putting theory into practice or sharpening a specific skill, and
5) negotiating skills.

Rewards for Mentors

Mentoring is a two-way exchange and mentors also benefit from the relationship. The biggest reward is knowing that one's hard-earned expertise will benefit the mentee. Many believe the mentor stands to profit even more than his or her mentee, especially if he or she is willing to learn.

There's a creativity in bright young persons that isn't always present in older folks. If a man or woman is reasonably flexible and listens well, he or she can pick up a lot from the younger man/woman. Mentoring can be a sort of modification of the aging process—the mentor exchanges his or her wisdom for new energy. A good mentee can make an older man/woman interested in things he or she thought he or she stopped caring about and livens up his or her life as he or she most needs it. (Nugent, 1980, p. 54)

Some Things Mentors Learn
From Economically Disadvantaged Children

In the summer workshops Torrance (1973) conducted for economically disadvantaged children, he was always surprised at how much the mentors/teachers learned from the children. In addition to the small group activities in drawing, sculpture, science, drama, creative writing, and story telling, each teacher/mentor was assigned to spend an hour each day with one or two children. They were to talk with these children, take a special interest in them, let the children teach them something, and let one thing lead to another. Many of them developed genuine mentor relationships.

The following are examples of the direct teachings reported by these 55 mentor/teachers:

- How to make a slingshot,
- How to tie a half hitch knot,
- How to climb a tree (I had always been afraid of heights),
- How to draw a profile of a man (I had never been able to do this),
- How to do a cannonball dive off a diving board,
- How to make a fishing pole from a stick, piece of nylon cord, safety pin, and small piece of metal,
- How to hitchhike in brainstorming,
- How and where to find fish bait,
- How to play checkers with some original rules,
- Precisely what to do during a tornado,
- "All" about berries, birds, and so forth,
- How to use a peach for fish bait,
- How to do various kinds of dances,

- How to play "Steal the Bacon,"
- How to ford a stream,
- How to make funny noises with my tongue,
- How to identify various kinds of fish, wild flowers, trees, insects, and so forth.

Many of the indirect learnings are things that we had tried to teach in the classroom during the two weeks prior to the workshop or that we had hoped they would learn through reading. We realized, of course, that there is a big difference between learning about something and "really" learning it. This is especially true of the efforts of middle class teachers and mentors to acquire the special understandings and skills necessary for helping disadvantaged children. The following are examples of the indirect learnings reported by teachers in this workshop.

- How to use non-verbal cues and to "read body English,"
- How to relax more and enjoy physical and human surroundings,
- How to understand the dialects of children from poverty backgrounds,
- How to enjoy a library more fully,
- How to listen more and talk less,
- How to get "totally" involved,
- Appreciation of the culture of poverty,
- That all children thrive on one-to-one interaction,
- That disadvantaged children have deep ideas though they may not be expressed in correct grammar,
- That disadvantaged children excel in brainstorming and problem solving,
- That approval and reinforcement cannot be delayed at times,
- That traditional direct approaches to controlling undesirable behavior are miserable failures with some disadvantaged children,
- That each person has his own "way" and needs to have a chance to use it,
- How cruel racial and poverty prejudice can be,

- That fear is a verbal retarder,
- How to tell when a child is not feeling well,
- That economically disadvantaged children want to be taught, can be taught, and will work willingly and hard at difficult mental tasks,
- How to be looser, more spontaneous, more demonstrative,
- That disadvantaged children like poetry and can write poetry,
- Not to try to fool them,
- Always have ready a second or third plan in case one does not work,
- How to admit ignorance about something that someone thinks I should know, and
- That the mentor's goals may not be the student's goals.

One thing that comes through very clearly in the descriptions of experiences in which children taught mentors/teachers is that disadvantaged children prize greatly these shared experiences in which they are respected and are able to give their teachers something of genuine value. The following report illustrates this important point.

> Mark and I shared many ideas, feelings, and experiences. Still we talked about one final adventure with a certain scientific value. We were going to catch some turtles which we discovered were abundant in two certain places on the Oconee River near the cemetery and the Boys' Club.
>
> On the last Friday, we took net and pail to the river. Mark was going to come down the river and, as the turtles saw him and evacuated the log on which they sunned, I was to net them as they rode the current downstream. It didn't work. We made three valiant efforts but failed. We each slipped while waist high and got soaked completely.
>
> In one place we almost ran into dangerously deep water. My wallet and watch were soaked. Mark nearly lost his glasses. He later scratched his leg. The turtle hunt failed. I was almost apologizing by saying how smart the turtles were, how good their vision, and so forth. Mark

responded in a way I'll never forget. He said it was the most exciting thing he's ever done. He would always remember it. And I wondered how Mark would cope with failure—he saw the success in it. It was our relationship, our shared experience.

Some of the teaching experiences reported might even be classed as psychotherapy—experiences which helped the teacher overcome a life-long fear or prejudice. The following quotation from one report illustrates such a result.

I'm afraid of heights and have been all my life. One afternoon Jack, Jackie, Julius, Carl, and I were exploring the roads behind Village Apartments. We came to the giant treehouse and observation tower. All wanted to explore it. I froze. I admitted being afraid, and the four of them began to coax me up the ladder. We reached the first level and my knees were so weak that I could barely stand up.

Jackie said, "See you can do it. There's nothing to be scared of." Jack echoed, "You're halfway there. Take my hand and I'll pull you up and Jackie, you push. Carl, you climb on up to help pull." I was panicking. I didn't know what to do. I closed my eyes but they began to urge me on. Finally after being coaxed for 10 minutes I started up the second ladder. I was so scared when I reached the top I was sure I would faint and be killed.

I survived and as we sat around on the observation ledge I found myself enjoying the experience. The children told me stories about how one time they were afraid but that it was "silly." We all laughed and joked and I really began to loosen up. I was still scared but it was bearable fear.

As the children pointed out the river we were overlooking, the cemetery, the other giant trees, the birds, the dogs below on the ground, the sky through the leaves, the swing below, and all the million and one beauties of nature, I reflected on my childhood and for the first time really realized just how silly it had been to be afraid of heights and just how much beauty I had missed from the ground. I had grown up looking through the trees, really a narrow perspective.

Some of the child-teaching episodes described by the adult teachers reveal that some economically disadvantaged children have quite sophisticated teaching skills and strategies. A skilled educational psychologist could hardly do better than 11-year-old Tami in the following report by one teacher.

What if a child teaches us something and unknowingly includes the things we try so hard to make ourselves do, such as heightening anticipation, encountering the unexpected, and so on? … Needless to say, when Tami offered to show me some crochet stitches, my anticipation was already considerably heightened. Tami and I both enjoy this type of work, and here was my chance to learn something new.

Tami brought her crochet hook on Monday, and instead of knitting, she began to show me the elementary, she assured me, chain stitch. I could make the loops all right, but when it came to pulling the crochet hook through the loops, my efforts sent Tami into great laughter. I think that perhaps it comes as a shock to school aged people when teacher can't do something right away. Tami encountered my unexpected clumsiness with a great deal of patience and reassurance—"I just know you'll get it this time, Beth"— and I did begin to improve.

Tuesday was the day, though. Tami brought a crocheted "book worm" to show me. This little thing can be smoothed flat to mark a place in a book, or it can be curled up to look as much like a worm as yarn possibly can. Might one call this "deepening expectations"? Tami, after being satisfied that I had mastered the chain stitch, set me to work on the book worm, with the understanding that I could work on it more before Thursday. Tami, I found, is a firm teacher. She expects me to apply myself to crocheting just as she applied herself to knitting. And I found I wouldn't dare let her down.

As for going "beyond the lesson," Tami told me about

another stitch that she wants to teach me on Thursday—a stitch used to crochet hats and scarves. She explained that the stitch is more difficult but assured me that if I would have the book worm done by Thursday, she would have no trouble teaching me the new stitch. Again, I know what she expects me to do, and I will do it. This has been something of an insight for me with regard to the ways in which a teacher's sureness of the student affects the student.

Tami was quick to praise me when I got the stitches right, and she corrected my work with confidence so that I would get it right. Of course, one may say that a child would naturally assume that an adult would be able to learn that which was being taught, but in this particular case my pulling that crochet hook through the loops was plain pitiful. The hook catches on things and is really quite frustrating—makes those big knitting needles a breeze. Tami remained cheerful, however, and I can truthfully say that my attempts might have exasperated a less determined and patient teacher. Being taught has certainly made me pay more careful attention than ever, and even more important, it has helped me know Tami in several new and exciting ways.

Mentors are motivated to assist mentees for a wide variety of reasons, both personal and professional. Chances are all of us have been a mentor, at least temporarily, for one reason or another. These relationships provide both immediate and long lasting benefits. Successful mentor relationships are mutually beneficial, create opportunities, and enhance learning which probably would not have occurred otherwise.

It is difficult to surmise what sustains a mentor relationship and results in mutual satisfaction. It seems certain that both persons in a mentor relationship must continue to grow and contribute to each other's growth. If children are oppressed by the myth that adults never make mistakes and always know all, they should be frankly told that it is a myth. They will grow and expand in unexpected ways when mentors give them opportunities and experiences that help them break through this myth.

Successful Mentor Relationships

It requires a real commitment of time and energy by the mentor and the mentee to create a successful mentor relationship. The most successful mentor relationships are entirely voluntary.

Approachability of the mentor is another important factor in a successful relationship. The mentee must feel comfortable enough in the relationship to ask questions, be honest, and share problems as they arise. There must be a climate of honesty and mutual respect as well as two-way communication.

For a successful relationship, the mentor must play many roles in the life of the mentee. One of the most powerful roles of the mentor is that of model. The mentor must "practice what he or she preaches." Mentors must be a living example of how they wish their mentees to be and act.

Another role is that of teacher. Mentors provide mentees with a gold mine of practical knowledge. Mentors share wisdom gained through actual life and work experiences. Mentoring at its best is a one-to-one learning experience.

A third very important role of a mentor is that of counselor. The mentor is in the mentee's corner, providing support, understanding, and encouragement. The mentor passes on interpersonal knowledge and skills as well as technical knowledge and skills.

CHAPTER 6
INTERGENERATIONAL
MENTOR/MENTEE
RELATIONSHIPS

In this chapter we provide ideas which have proven successful in mentor relationships involving various age groups. Intergenerational learning is very powerful in enhancing communication between different generations and in practicing the skills of interdependence. Both the mentor and the mentee have strengths and, most likely, their strengths

I'LL CHOOSE HER! SHE REMINDS ME OF MY GRAMMA!

are different. By learning things together each can contribute to the relationship from their particular strengths, thus creating a richer, more interdependent relationship.

Adult Mentor
and Primary Aged Mentee

Some ideas which have proven successful in this type of mentor relationship include:

1) arranging for the mentee to see the mentor at work,
2) discovering a natural interest of the mentee and pursuing it,
3) helping the mentee fall in love with something,
4) listening to the mentee's stories, fantasy or true,
5) listening to the mentee's songs and poems,
6) showing the mentee strange objects, innovative or unusual processes,
7) finding out how the mentee investigates or explores ideas or projects,
8) having the mentee look at something in different ways and conditions, and
9) encouraging the mentee to look at something twice, reading something twice, especially if the mentee expresses further interest.

Adult Mentor and Upper Elementary Aged Mentee

Suggestions for enhancing this relationship are:
1) find out about the mentee's creative achievements,
2) recognize the mentee for these achievements,
3) support the dreams of the mentee,
4) find out the talents of the mentee and make him or her aware of them,
5) suggest participation in the Future Problem Solving or Odyssey of the Mind Program (for more information see Programs for Creative Development), and
6) encourage participation in suitable clubs, organizations, and activities.

Adult Mentor and Intermediate Aged Mentee

Ideas for cultivating this mentor relationship include:
1) find out about the mentee's creative achievements,

2) find out about the mentee's hobbies and leisure activities,
3) give the mentee information about appropriate summer jobs, camps, or other summer activities,
4) participate with the mentee (you or someone nearer) in some kind of investigation or other project,
5) help the mentee obtain advanced skills, and
6) help him or her in preparing for local science fairs or other local programs.

Adult Mentor
and Upper High School Aged Mentee

Juniors and seniors in high school are faced with very important decisions about their immediate and long range futures. Some helpful ideas for this mentor relationship are:

1) help the mentee to evaluate colleges, technical schools, other post-secondary schooling, military training, or on-the-job training programs,
2) help the mentee in applying for scholarships or other financial aid,

3) help in preparing for tests used in college admission and scholarships,
4) assist in the planning and preparation for science fairs, academic competitions, auditions, and job interviews,
5) help get some of the mentee's creative ideas produced, marketed, or published,
6) certify the mentee's expertise in areas which are not certified, such as some new skill, occupation, or special expertise, and
7) publicly praise original, unusual work in demand.

Adult Mentor and Adult Mentee

This type of mentor relationship occurs on the job, in the home, with parents, in an organization or club, or in a professional organization. Some suggestions for fostering this type of relationship include:

1) offer the mentee further training or study opportunities,
2) suggest the possibility of further educational study,
3) recommend the mentee for a promotion, tenure, or new jobs,
4) assist the mentee in preparing for the entrance exams and obtaining an adviser,
5) publicly praise good, original work,
6) help the mentee achieve desired certification,

7) certify the expertness of the mentee, and

8) assist the mentee in making changes in occupations; assist mentee in assessing him or herself, identifying possible new occupations, acquiring needed skills, and making contact with employers.

Implication of Intergenerational Differences in Mentoring in the Culture of Poverty

Now let us consider the implications of all of the above for mentoring in the culture of poverty. What are the differences between mentoring the economically disadvantaged and the affluent at each of the stages described in the foregoing?

In the affluent family, the primary aged child might accompany his or her parents to work and would usually be expected to follow the same kind of work as one or both parents. In the economically disadvantaged family, the primary aged child's parents might not have jobs or their jobs would likely be of a type that not even the parents would want him or her to follow. The economically disadvantaged child is discouraged from discovering and pursuing their natural interests. It would only be with a mentor that he or she could even consider it. Usually the economically disadvantaged child is not allowed to recognize the possibility of being in love with any kind of work. Only with a mentor would he or she know of this possibility. Only in such a relationship can he or she have anyone to listen to his or her stories, songs, and poems.

Only in a mentor relationship would a primary aged child likely have access to strange objects or innovative or unusual processes. Only in such a relationship would he or she be able to investigate or explore ideas and projects, deliberately look at something in different ways, or be encouraged to look at or read something twice—or more.

Among economically disadvantaged upper elementary children, creative achievements are not usually recognized or even acknowledged. Thus, these children have no way of knowing their strengths. Frequently, a mentor is the only one in a position of helping them to do this. This is not true of affluent children. Their parents, friends, and coaches recognize and acknowledge such achievements. The economically disadvantaged upper elementary youngster has to keep dreams to him or herself, unless there is a mentor who will listen and encourage. His or her parents will say, "You have no chance of being anything like that!" Likewise, no one is going to find out their talents, suggest that they participate in the Future Problem Solving Program, Odyssey of the Mind Program, or the like. He or she might participate in the Invent America Program, if his or her school participates and includes all enrollees. Even then, he or she might need a mentor to help do the research about its uniqueness and marketability and finding the materials for building a prototype of his or her invention. The mentor might also need to encourage participation in suitable organizations and help acquire whatever is necessary for participation.

Similarly, the intermediate aged economically disadvantaged youth would have about the same difficulty in recognizing his or her creative achievements as the upper elementary school youth. Their hobbies and leisure activities might be revealing and give clues to what they really love. Of course, the economically disadvantaged youngster might have little or no time for hobbies and leisure activities because they have to work, help care for the younger family members or even care for elderly or ill family members. In fact, they may even have to drop out of school because of this. If there is time, the mentor might give information about appropriate summer jobs or camps, investigate some project, help them obtain information about college scholarships, help them obtain some higher level skill, or the like. Or, they might need help in obtaining needed materials for a science fair project.

The economically disadvantaged upper high school youth is certain to need help in evaluating colleges, technical schools or other post-secondary schools, military training, or on-the-job training programs. The mentor can also help them in applying for scholarships and other financial aid. They are likely to badly need help in preparing for tests used in college admission and scholarships. In some cases, the mentor needs to give assistance in preparing them for interviews, auditions, or preparing portfolios of art works, creative writing, and so forth, depending upon what their talent is. Frequently, mentors may need to give help in getting their mentees products produced, marketed, or published. If the mentee has gone ahead and developed an unusual or new skill or expertise, the mentor might validate or certify it. By all means, the mentor should publicly praise original, unusual work in demand.

The economically disadvantaged adult will need help in finding further training or study opportunities. The mentor may be in a position to recommend him or her for promotion, tenure, or new jobs. The adult mentee may need help in preparing for entrance examinations and in obtaining an adviser. Above all, the mentor needs to publicly acknowledge and praise good, original work. The mentee may still need guidance in achieving the desired certification or being certified in a new area of expertise. The adult mentor may also help in changing occupations. He or she may need help in assessing his or her skills, likes and dislikes, identifying possible new occupations, acquiring new skills needed, and making contacts with possible new employers. Successful mentoring moves the mentee from the role of dependent learner to that of independent learner.

Two of the most frequently mentioned changes in direction of the mentoring relationship were the colleague and friend relationships.

The mentor serves as a role model initially. As the mentee matures, the mentor and mentee become real colleagues, with the mentee contributing to the knowledge and growth of the mentor. With the increasing rate of change, expansion of knowledge, and the creation of new technology, this aspect of the mentor-mentee relationship is certain to become more crucial and frequent.

Mentors of economically disadvantaged children are sometimes drawn into a mentor relationship with one or both of the mentee's parents. Such relationships may result in an upgrading of the parents' occupation. When this happens the mentee benefits because the parents can then afford more advantages for the mentee. In fact, George Witt (1971) reported that this happened quite frequently in his program in New Haven, CT, already discussed in an earlier chapter.

Mentors come in all ShAPES and SIZES

CHAPTER 7
MENTOR AS LIAISON

A mentor must truly be interested in the growth and welfare of his or her mentee, and therefore, must communicate with the mentee's significant others as well as the school system, if the child is of school age. A mentor usually is thrust into the role of middleman between the mentee and the home environment and the mentee, home environment, and the school system. Generally, the communication between the mentee and these institutions is poor and is resulting in alarming dropout rates.

This chapter describes some strategies for a mentor to use in establishing a beneficial partnership between the "family" and the school system on behalf of the mentee.

Mentors and Parents/Guardians

The traditional concept of "family" is less likely to reflect the true nature of the economically disadvantaged family. More and more disadvantaged families are being headed by single females. According to Moore and Pachon (1985), female-headed families are much more likely to be living in poverty than more typical, male-headed families.

It is important for the mentor to gain an understanding of the mentee's family situation. Many times the mother may be out of the house a lot, leaving a grandmother or other relative to supervise the child. It is, therefore, important for the mentor to communicate a "we're all in this together" attitude in characterizing the mentor-mentee relationship.

Wood and Geisman (1989) have cited three overriding principles in developing a beneficial partnership with the mentee's family:

1) relate to family members in such a way as to help them to begin to feel safe and supported, sometimes verbally, but more usually behaviorally; communicate courtesy and respect; relate to strengths rather than inadequacies; appreciate and admire their strengths;

2) be honest and up-front; be interested in what family members see as their pressing and important problems; and

3) relate to them as a family group; develop a relationship of partnership in finding ways to improve their situations.

Mentors and the School System

Twenty-seven percent of all children in the U.S. drop out of school before graduation and nearly 50 percent are from economically disadvantaged households (Woodkowski & Jaynes, 1990). Additionally, youth who are not members of the social, cultural, and educational mainstream, approximately 29 percent of school aged youth, account for more than half of all juveniles in public custody (Allen-Hagen, 1988).

Virtually all children are born with the motivation to learn and are excited about beginning their school careers. However, upon entering, school children are expected to ignore their previous learning strategies of experimenting, manipulating, and experiencing

learning in favor of verbal learning almost exclusively. For children from economically disadvantaged backgrounds this new form of learning is foreign to them and they are unclear as to how this new form of learning relates to their everyday lives. They are unable to see that school learning leads to something worthwhile, which leaves them unmotivated and unexcited about learning.

Mentors can aid a mentee who is still in school by providing experiences that give him or her opportunities to use what is learned and to show interest in what he or she has learned rather than on the grades made. Mentors can also assist in developing a positive relationship between the school and the home.

Too often parents/guardians and teachers of economically disadvantaged children communicate only when there is a problem. Parents who may have experienced rejection or exclusion in school may resist attending school meetings or functions and decide to stay away because of their past negative experiences. School personnel may interpret the absence of these parents as a sign of disinterest and may feel justified in not continuing to reach out to the parents whom they have judged to be apathetic. This, in turn, may reinforce the parent's decision to keep their distance. Time pressures, multiple responsibilities, and unspoken assumptions and expectations all contribute to putting off efforts to build a positive relationship.

Mentors can aid parents in their communication with the school system by:

1) helping parents/guardians respond to invitations to school events, requests for information or assistance, even if the response means letting the teachers know that such participation may be difficult;

2) helping parents/guardians take advantage of opportunities to learn about their child's education;

3) helping parents/guardians encourage and respect their children in their scholastic endeavors;

4) helping parents/guardians express compassion and beliefs that their children can excel; and

5) helping parents/guardians to gain information about available community resources and to focus on their children's strengths rather than weaknesses.

Mentors may also help parents/guardians and teachers in developing a positive relationship by reminding them that (Woodkowski & Jaynes, 1990):
  1) both are concerned and competent people,
  2) both are making their best efforts for the good of the child,
  3) both have pressures and responsibilities, and
  4) both need support in their efforts toward problem solving.

CHAPTER 8
EVALUATION/FEEDBACK
FOR CREATIVE
IDEAS/PRODUCTS

Successes with Ideas and Products

Creativity involves dealing with ideas and products. First, one must come up with ideas. Ideas come to anyone who is willing to look for them. According to Hanks and Parry (1983), a universal law which applies to all existence is: If you don't need something, you won't be very motivated to create or learn it.

Creative behavior occurs in the process of becoming sensitive to or aware of problems, deficiencies, gaps in knowledge, missing elements, disharmonies, and so on; bringing together in new relationships available information; defining the difficulty or identifying the missing elements; searching for solutions, making guesses, or formulating hypotheses about the problem or deficiencies; testing and retesting them; perfecting them; and finally communicating the results. This is a natural, healthy human process. Strong human motivations are at work at each stage.

Sensing an incompleteness, disharmony, or problem arouses tension or motivation. The mentee is uncomfortable, curious, excited. Since he or she has no adequate learned response or his or her habitual ways of responding are inadequate, the mentee searches both in his or her own memory storehouse and in other sources such as books, the experiences of others, and information about the difficulty. From these, he or she tries to identify the actual gap in information or to define the problem. This achieved, he or she searches for possible alternative solutions, diagnosing, manipulating, rearranging, building onto previous experience, and making guesses or approximations. Until these guesses or hypotheses are tested, modified, and retested, the mentee is still motivated to continue the process. He or she continues trying to perfect his or her solution until it is logically and aesthetically satisfying. The tension remains unrelieved, however, until the learner communicates his or her discoveries, solutions, or productions. This is when mentors need to listen.

Reviewing Products As a Mentor

At this point, the mentee communicates his or her idea or product to the mentor. In reviewing the idea or product, it is crucial for the mentor to find at least one element of the idea or product which he or she can honestly praise. There is always something to praise. This is much more important in mentoring economically disadvantaged children and youth than more affluent ones.

When mentees produce something there is a part of themselves in that production. Criticism in the usual manner can be taken as a personal indictment against the mentee. It does not take many of these to convince the mentee that he or she does not have good ideas. There may be many faults with it, but if he or she receives some acceptance, through praise, then he or she will not set up defenses to ward off attack and is more willing to examine his or her ideas in a meaningful, constructive manner.

In searching for the positive:

- *Look at the parts that contribute to the whole.* One may show terrific insight even if the end product itself is not praiseworthy.
- *Look at the finished product.* Many mentees can stumble around working through a thought process, seemingly muddled, and emerge with a wonderful product. That finished product should be praised first, before the parts are picked apart.
- *The praise should be specific and refer to an identifiable element.* "The wheel on your machine looks strong and sturdy" is better than "You drew such a nice machine."

Feedback is a necessary part of learning and the growth process. It should be "gentle" and couched in terms that are nonthreatening. Criticism should not be ruled out as it is dishonest to allow mentees to feel that what they have done is sufficient if it is not. In fact, mentees often lose confidence in mentors who accept everything; who never show belief that they can reach greater insights.

Some helpful prefaces to criticism are:

- "More colorful words would express your ideas more clearly. They are important, and you want people to understand what you are saying."
- "If you make the character more active, it will give your picture the feeling you are trying to express."
- "If you make the base out of sturdier material, your invention will last longer."
- "This is a good start. Explain the process more completely and people will really be able to use your ideas."

Developing Product Improvements

After you have a number of suggestions about the idea or product, it is necessary to evaluate them to determine which can improve the idea of product. In order to look closely and critically at the idea or product Isaksen and Treffinger (1985, p. 7–11) provide the following tips for choosing the best options:

- compare many alternatives;
- compare desires (wants) with demands (needs);
- examine the "pros" and "cons" of several ideas;
- narrow the options to a manageable group;
- determine the strengths and weaknesses of ideas or products, to help "build" or develop their best features;
- screen ideas for possible modifications and improvements;
- reject options you do not wish to consider further; and
- select or decide upon your most promising possibilities.

Some important questions to ask are:
- Will it cost too much?
- Is it too time consuming?
- Will it work?
- Do I like it?
- Is it useful or beneficial?

Completing, Marketing, or Putting Aside Products

It is time to put the plan into action or put it aside in order to pursue new interests. After carefully analyzing the idea or product, you may decide it is too costly, too time consuming, and so forth. If this is the case, you may want to put this idea or product aside and get involved with another.

However, if after careful consideration you decide to complete the idea or product, it is advisable to set up an immediate action plan (what you are going to do in the next 24 hours), a short-range plan (what you are going to do in the next month), and a long-range plan for the next six months to two years.

The long range plan will include marketing of the idea and product. This phase begins with research.

- Is a similar idea or product being produced by someone else? How is it doing or how did it do?
- Define your market. Who would this idea or product appeal to? Where do they shop? How do they live?
- What is the idea or product going to cost to produce? What will the selling price be?

Once you have answered these questions you will have a general feel for the possible success of the idea or product. Next, you will need to build a prototype. When creating a prototype it is very important to enlist the services of a graphic artist if you are not one. The mentor may be able to help the mentee find someone.

After completion of the prototype, you may try to sell the idea or product to someone else. Before you talk to someone else about purchasing or producing your idea or product, be sure you have it protected by obtaining a patent, copyright, or trademark. Unless you know someone who is interested in your idea or product, it is *very* difficult to get someone to listen.

If you do not find a publisher or manufacturer who is interested in your idea or product, one option is self-publishing or self-manufacturing. You may not want this as a future career, but it is vital that you conduct at least preliminary tests on the appeal of your idea or product. The data from test marketing are essential when trying to convince a publisher or manufacturer to buy your license, idea, or product. Test marketing will provide further feedback on the strengths and weaknesses of the idea or product. It will also give you an idea of the obstacles to be faced in marketing the idea or product.

If the test marketing yields good results and you have enough money or can find a supporter, you might want to hire a marketing specialist to work with your product or idea. Be careful when talking to promoters and marketing specialists. Do your homework on their track records and be sure they are reputable. As a matter of fact, it is important to know the background and track records of any business or individual with whom you will be working. This information is usually available in libraries, in annual reports, and from professional organizations.

At any point in this long process you may decide that it is not feasible to continue with the idea or product. Persistence and hard work are the key factors in successfully creating and marketing any idea or product. Throughout this entire process, the mentor must assist the mentee in solving problem after problem and in making contacts, as well as assisting in finding financial support.

CHAPTER 9
ONE THING LEADS
TO ANOTHER

Evolution of Ideas into Interests Expanded Beyond Mentor's Capabilities or Interests

Mentees drift away from their mentors when they find the mentor too limited in perspective and unable to look beyond present trends and past successes.

The evolution of ideas created in a mentor relationship may send the mentee and mentor down different paths, in which case their interests may become different. It is both the mentor's and the mentee's responsibility to begin communicating with each other on new ideas, goals, or products or mutually decide to terminate the relationship.

The Mentor and Mentee Say Good-bye

At some point in time every mentor relationship ends. There are many factors which contribute to the ending of a mentor relationship. Some of these factors are death, geographical separation, career change, changes in philosophies and outlooks on life, family responsibilities, and so on.

The spiritual aspects of the mentor relationship may continue long after the actual relationship. Jack Presbury (1986), in his poem "Icarus" (written to E. Paul Torrance, the late astronaut Christa McAuliffe, and other great Teacher-Challengers of the world), writes:

Like Icarus,
The Challengers
Are never dead and gone.
They're always awaiting somewhere
To cheer the children on.

This "cheering one on" may be in the form of books, instructional materials, inventions, charities, foundations, and so forth. created by retired mentors and deceased mentors or by mentees in honor of their mentors.

Referring Mentee to Different Mentor

If a mentee's interests have evolved to a point that the mentor does not feel capable of or interested in meeting the needs of the mentee's new interests, it is time for the mentor to pass the mentee on to a more interested and capable mentor in the new area of interest.

The transition period affects mentor relationships differently. The more caring and mutual respect involved in the relationship, the more difficult the transition may be. During a transition it is important to focus on the positive aspects of the present and future relationships.

A successful transition is facilitated by a healthy sense of change. The change should not cause fear rather an excitement of new ideas and experiences. The transition has a better chance of being successful if the mentor and mentee look at it as a positive change and an opportunity for growth.

When a mentor refers a mentee to a different mentor it is important for the mentee to learn everything he or she can about the new mentor from the old mentor. Generally, the original mentor will call or write the new mentor about the mentee. The new mentor usually notifies the original mentor as to whether he or she feels capable or is interested in assisting the mentee. From this point on, the responsibility for the new mentor relationship transfers to the mentee and the new mentor. It is their responsibility to begin communicating with each other on new ideas, goals, or products.

Sources of Mentors and Children and Young People from the Culture of Poverty who Need Mentors

When mentors make referrals to another mentor from what sources can they seek someone to continue the mentoring process? The mentor may know of someone personally who can assume this role. It is indeed fortunate if this is the case.

There are a variety of such sources and some of them have already been described in this book. There are, in many locations, organizations or clubs for this specific purpose. One already mentioned several times is Black Men Mentoring Black Boys. These groups include lawyers, judges, doctors, police officers, merchants, salesmen, and the like. In some school systems, chambers of commerce and other civic organizations are in positions to help. Another source is retired people. In most localities, there are organizations of retired teachers, including university and professional school faculty. Most of them are eager to still be needed by young people.

There are always plenty of children and young people in the culture of poverty who need mentoring. Besides schools, there are the courts, Boys and Girls Clubs, and similar organizations. An overlooked source is alternative schools, and this will be discussed as an example.

Alternative schools are a rich resource of youngsters needing mentoring, especially youngsters who come from the culture of poverty. Many school systems have organized alternative schools as an alternative to expulsion. Students are sent to alternative schools when they are unable to adjust to regular schools and their behavior cannot be tolerated. Teachers and administrators in these schools are frequently able to establish good relationships with these students and, to some extent, become temporary mentors, helping them find long-time mentor relationships and make a real difference in their lives.

According to Christy Oglesby in her feature article in the *Atlanta Journal* (September 26, 1996, p. C8), there are now more than 15,000 students in Georgia's alternative schools. These students are plagued by health, home, and classroom problems and welcome the second chance alternative schools give them. However, they need the help and support that a mentor could give them. There are many success stories of economically disadvantaged youngsters who experience alternative schools (Weiss, September 26, 1996, p. C8). However, the teachers, administrators, and mentors are not without risk. One tragic example is related by Michael Weiss in his feature article in the *Atlanta Journal*, the story of the shooting death of the beloved English teacher, Horace Pierpoint Morgan.

Dr. Morgan was a dedicated teacher, wanted "to make a difference," and he had made a difference in the lives of many youngsters (Cumming, September 25, 1996, *Atlanta Journal*, p. C1). He had tried to make a difference in the life of his slayer. Fortunately, this was described as an isolated incident. The fact remains that the teachers, administrators, counselors, and mentors of these youngsters are always left at risk.

Mentoring in the culture of poverty has usually been as rewarding to the mentor as to the young persons being mentored. Mentors learn and experience as well as teach. One volunteer mentor working with a fourth grade boy said, "I love it. I like having someone to pal around with. It's good to have his perspective on things, which is totally different from what I'm used to." Another mentor of a fifth grade girl enjoyed going to the library and both of them selecting books, visiting the art museum, and going to the YWCA. They both learned so much from one another.

CHAPTER 10
EXAMPLES AND IDEAS
FOR MENTOR PROGRAMS

Examples of Mentor Relationships

Mentor relationships exist in an endless variety of settings, circumstances, combinations, and personnel. Briefly, we will describe some differing examples of successful mentor relationships.

The earliest mentor for a child is usually a parent, grandparent, or other closely connected family member. Parents and other family members are particularly effective in assisting children in the development of their creative strengths and potentials. In many rural areas, parents and family members are thrust into the mentor roles due to lack of resources and specialists.

This was the case for Abigail Adams, mother of John Quincy Adams (the sixth president of the United States). Their town had lost its only school teacher, so Abigail became her son's teacher. She taught John to read and write and further stimulated his learning by him watching her single-handedly run their estate during the difficult times leading up to and through the American Revolution. Abigail's mentoring style was firmness combined with kindness.

An essential function of the parental or familial mentor is to build the child's self-esteem and provide support. Thomas Edison was labeled "addled" (retarded) after three months of schooling when he was 7 years old. His mother resented and rejected this evaluation. She decided to keep him home and teach him herself. She sensed that the best approach was to let him follow his own interests. She led him through various subjects until she introduced him to science. At that point, his mind ignited and he started teaching himself. Later Edison said that his mother was his inspiration and strength. She understood him and let him explore and experience learning on his own.

Fathers as well as mothers can be powerful mentors for their children. One creative woman, in Torrance's 22-year longitudinal study (1984), called her father her most important mentor and wrote:

> He taught me the value of honesty. He is my friend. He listens to me as I do him. I value his judgment and we help each other in our work. He encourages me to try whatever I would like. He never condemns me or berates me and knows that I would help him in any way I can. (p. 16)

The "parent as mentor" role offers parents/guardians the opportunities to grow creatively with their children and to "keep in touch" with what their children are doing. Important bonding between a child and his or her familial mentor can produce strength and courage and love for both individuals.

Many times a mentor unknowingly provides support, encouragement, or leadership which may prove crucial to a mentee's career. Joseph Michelotti, MD, was one of six children his immigrant Italian parents had managed to send to top colleges and graduate schools. (Three became doctors, two were lawyers and one was a physicist.) When he and his brothers and sisters were children, their mother was their mentor. From the very beginning she urged her children to think big and constantly encouraged and praised them. She always said that success wasn't just making money; success was doing something positive for others (Michelotti, 1991).

Stevie Wonder was given a harmonica when he was very young by a barber who noticed that Stevie liked music. Later, Stevie took to the piano and organ and began singing. When he was 11 years old, Ronnie White of the Miracles heard of Stevie through a younger brother who was a friend of Stevie's cousin. White listened to Stevie's music, liked what he heard and took him to the local Black recording company, Hitsville USA. The company's president, Barry Gordy Jr., was impressed with Stevie's voice and his adeptness with various instruments, signed him to a contract, and changed his name to something more marketable and more descriptive of the prodigy. The rest is history (Slater, 1977).

Mentors, especially the first mentor, are very important and can sometimes, without knowing it, change someone's life. Flip Wilson came from a broken, poverty-stricken home of 18 brothers and sisters who ended up in three foster homes before the age of 7. In school, there was a "white" teacher who showed special interest in him. He was half a grade or more behind because he had moved so much, but she told him he was a bright student and put him up with the kids his own age. Wilson did everything he could to prove to her that he was a bright student and continued to strive to prove himself from then on.

Generally, mentors are role models which the mentee tries to emulate. This often occurs with children who observe or encounter someone and "fall in love with" whatever this person is doing, saying, or being. All of us have heard of a young child who "falls in love with" the circus and chooses a career as a clown or acrobat.

It is very difficult, especially for children, not to put the mentor on a pedestal or in an ivory tower. When this does happen, it usually means the beginning of the end or the end of the mentor relationship. The mentee's expectations are so high that the mentor cannot possibly live up to them. Also, the imposed expectations may not be congruent with the mentor's ideas and beliefs. Thus when the relationship becomes unbalanced in this manner, it ceases to be a growing relationship. This relationship will stagnate and eventually die if left unbalanced.

> I respect him. I care about his well being. However, if I were to see him again, I would make it clear that we were still friends, but not mentor to mentee. Circumstances before he left were very difficult and disillusioning to me and I still hurt from this. (Torrance, 1984, p. 26–27)

It is difficult to surmise what sustains mentor relationships that result in mutual satisfaction. It seems certain that both individuals in a mentor relationship must continue to grow, must continue to contribute to each other's growth, and must maintain clear channels of communication between each other.

Mentor Program Ideas and Examples

Mentor programs are not a new phenomenon and have been increasing. In 1968, George Witt developed a program for a group

of gifted, inner-city, disadvantaged Black children who were identified on the basis of their creativity. Various kinds of sponsors or
mentors were arranged for both the children and their families. The
children were moved from their ghetto schools to mainstream public schools and later were provided scholarships to first-rate private
schools. Many of their parents and older siblings were assisted in
upgrading their educational and career skills which resulted in both
acquiring better jobs. The competencies which they attained were
an outgrowth of activities which focused on their creative positives
rather than deliberate attempts to develop those competencies.

Witt (1971) provides useful clues for intervention programs
attempting to implement this approach. The characteristics are as
follows:

1) Be clearly structured but flexible and open-ended.
2) Provide opportunities to be rewarded for solving problems.
3) Be viewed by one and all in a positive light.
4) Be tangible; and have many activities conducted in the
   homes.
5) Have enough competent adults in charge to minimize the
   need for the jeering and quarreling.
6) Continue controls indefinitely.
7) Involve exciting people from the inner-city and non-inner
   city.
8) Design all learning experiences so that exciting perceptual-
   motor experiences precede, accompany, and follow cognitive growth.
9) Be intimately coordinated by a director expert in individual,
   group, and community dynamics.
10) Provide for the support, control, and involvement of the
    children's families, parents, and siblings.

More recent examples of innovative mentor programs include
the Linking Lifetimes program, a program which includes 140
older adult mentors and nearly 200 young people in 12 sites across
the country. The program combines the resources of older persons
with the needs of at-risk middle school students and youth in juvenile offender programs.

Another mentor program, which targets potential dropouts, is the Dade County, FL, public school's Intergenerational Law Advocacy Program. The project's goal is to help economically disadvantaged students advocate for themselves and their elders on issues that matter to both generations, such as health care, crime prevention, and public transportation. The program reaches 2,500 students in 24 schools throughout the county.

Based on five years of summer workshops with disadvantaged children, Torrance (1977) offers the following guidelines for nurturing and developing giftedness in economically disadvantaged youth:

1) Emphasis should be placed on the value of diversity and attention should be given to those kinds of giftedness which are valued by the particular culture to which a person belongs.

2) Creativeness should always be one of the criteria in searching for giftedness in the economically disadvantaged, because:
   a) creativity is a key characteristic of almost every person who has made outstanding social contributions, and
   b) creativity is one of the greatest and most common strengths of groups from the culture of poverty in the U.S.

3) Creativity is a multivariate phenomenon and therefore a variety of kinds of giftedness should be considered in the discovery and nurturance process.

4) The creative positives should be used in designing learning experiences and activities.

5) There should be avoidance of unreasonable financial demands. Stress should be placed on improvisation with commonplace materials, the use of natural phenomena, and access to public facilities, such as libraries, zoos, playgrounds, museums, parks, and public buildings.

6) Learning activities should be planned and executed as to help culturally different children cope with and grow out of any feelings of alienation. This will involve the development of pride in their strengths and opportunities for sharing the fruits of their strengths with others.

I LIKE DRAWING PONIES. WHO CARES ABOUT PONY PICTURES? I MIGHT AS WELL DRAW FIRE HYDRANTS

THEY KINDA LOOK LIKE US DAWGS

Summary

Mentoring is a creative endeavor where there must be a willingness to let one thing lead to another. It is a relationship which is entered into with trust and sincere desires for growth and learning. Each mentor relationship has the possibility for growing into a deep and caring one. There may even be a certain "magic" to the relationship.

Those who organize and foster mentor programs also should recognize that the mentor in a relationship may in time become a friend, teacher, competitor, lover, or father/mother figure. If the relationship is a deep and caring one (and this seems to be a major characteristic of a genuine mentor relationship), any of these relationships may evolve. However, because of the caring nature, the outcomes are not likely to be harmful.

There is also a need for mentor program organizers, as well as mentors and mentees, to be aware of the common obstacles to continuing, enduring mentor relationships. These include the frequently intimidating nature of some mentor relationships, setting too fast a pace and not respecting the natural pace of the mentee, making sacrifices to personal integrity, sex role barriers, racial barriers, behavior disapproved by the mentor or mentee, an incompatible philosophy of life of either party, aversion to institution or social systems to which the mentor belongs, feelings of threat to the status quo ignited by the mentee and feelings of hurt, mistreatment, or rejection.

Attention should be directed to the possible use of mentors for young children, especially creatively gifted ones from economically disadvantaged families. Without such attention, these children are likely to sacrifice their giftedness by the time they emerge from the primary grades.

Schools as well as businesses and industries need to expand the pool from which they recruit mentors. While there is a need for mentors with a future orientation, there is also a need to have them with an historical orientation. Young people with a future orientation may lack some of the power and prestige of the usual pool of mentors. However, mentors influence the images of the future of their mentees and it would be foolhardy not to recognize and develop this aspect of mentoring. Retired persons in business and industry, grandparents and other retired persons in school and families provide another pool of possible mentors. Virginia Ehrlich (1983) called attention to the potential of grandparents as mentors for young children. She urged parents to use the specialized knowledge of grandparents. She also maintains that grandparents will exert enormous energy locating special information to share with children.

These are some indications that a new and potentially important role may be emerging for mentors. A considerable number of mentees attain their expertise through self-directed learning and/or a kind of apprenticeship with the assistance of a mentor. Since this expertise was not attained through a college or other accredited agency, there exists a new set of problems related to the validation of the expertise. In some cases, mentors have been able to certify the expertise of mentees through personal contacts or recommendations. This may become an increasing trend as change accelerates and as the attainment of professional expertise increasingly occurs through self-directed learning and experiential learning.

The following set of guidelines has been formulated for mentors and mentees. These are the most important things we can do to continue to grow creatively.

The Future of Mentoring

As we have already pointed out, the 1990s have been characterized by a growing interest in mentoring in general, mentoring the young, and mentoring in the culture of poverty in particular. Without the benefit of government support, mentoring has already shown that there is a large pool of people who are available— retired teachers, senior citizens, civic organizations, special clubs, church organizations, and business organizations.

Georgia's Governor Zell Miller made one of the earlier initiatives to establish mentor programs in middle schools. At the time, his proposal met so much opposition from the State Superintendent of Schools that he gave up. Governor Miller had had a mentor who helped him turn his life around, and he wanted children in today's schools to have this advantage. Some Georgia schools went ahead with mentoring programs. Throughout this book, we have reported some of the results, particularly in Athens and Atlanta. This was accomplished through the cooperation of the school systems and community organizations. There have been notable initiatives in other states. For example, Governor Pete Wilson of California has established a program to get 250,000 California youngsters into a mentoring relationship by the year 2000 (Powell, 1977).

Manifesto for Children

1. Don't be afraid to fall in love with something and pursue it with intensity.

2. Know, understand, take pride in, practice, develop, exploit, and enjoy your greatest strengths.

3. Learn to free yourself from the expectations of others and to walk away from the games they impose on you. Free yourself to play your own game.

4. Find a great teacher or mentor who will help you.

5. Don't waste energy trying to be well rounded.

6. Do what you love and can do well.

7. Learn the skills of interdependence.

We believe that the Summit for Our Future held in April, 1997, has given an unprecedented boost to mentoring in the culture of poverty. General Colin Powell (1997), who served as general coordinator of the Summit, with Presidents Clinton, Bush, Ford, and Carter, wrote that in his travels throughout the United States since his retirement, he had seen too many children and young people who are desperately in need of the basic essentials to becoming successful adults. He stated that the results are children giving birth to children, drug use, violence, crime, and undisciplined behavior in school. He gave a list of five fundamental resources that will lead to success. At the head of his list is "an ongoing relationship with a caring adult or mentor."

General Powell (1997, p. 5) enumerated some of the commitments already made to do something about it. Big Brothers and Big Sisters plan to increase the number of children to be mentored from 100,000 to 200,000 by the end of the decade. The organization 100 Black Men of America has committed to mentor 120,000 youngsters over the next three years. The National Council of University Women will deploy an additional 150,000 mentors and tutors. These are only a few of the commitments that have already been made. Although there have been detractors of the Summit, we believe that it will give mentoring in the culture of poverty a tremendous boost.

The authors hope that what we have provided will help mentors of the economically disadvantaged deal successfully with these problems and achieve their potentialities and find something that they will love.

REFERENCES

Allen-Hagen, B. (1988, October). Public juvenile facilities, 1987: Children in custody. *Juvenile Justice Bulletin.*

Atkinson, D. R., Morten, G., & Sue, D. W. (1983). *Counseling American minorities: A cross-cultural perspective* (2nd ed.). Dubuque, IA: Wm. C. Brown.

Bova, V. M., & Phillips, R. J. (1984). Mentoring as a learning experience from adults. *Journal of Teacher Education, 35*(4), 195–207.

Close, J. J. (1990). *No one to call me home.* Chicago, IL: Mission of Our Lady of Mercy.

Collins, N. W. (1983). *Professional women and their mentors.* Englewood Cliffs, NJ: Prentice-Hall.

Cox, B. (1996, May 13). Judge volunteers as local mentor. *Athens Banner Herald, 165*(95), 1.

Crabbe, A. (1981). Creating a brighter future: An update on the Future Problem Solving Program. *Journal for the Education of the Gifted, 5*(1), 2–11.

Ehrlich, V. (August, 1983). Grandparents and gifted children. *Gifted Children Newsletter, 4*(7), 1–3, 13.

Hall, V. M., & Wessel, J. A. (1987, June 14). Wise counseling by a mentor can greatly enrich a career. *Atlanta Journal/Atlanta Constitution,* 57.

Isaksen, S. G., & Treffinger, D. J. (1985). *Creative problem solving: The basic course.* Buffalo, NY: Bearly Limited.

Jeffers, C. (1961). *Living poor: A participant observer study of priorities and choices.* Ann Arbor, MI: Ann Arbor Publishers.

Karnes, F., & Riley, T. (1996). Competitions: developing and nurturing talents. *Gifted Child Today, 19*(2), 14–15, 49.

May, R. (1939). *The art of counseling.* Nashville, TN: Cokesbury Press.

Micklus, C. S. (1988). *Make learning fun!* Glassboro, NJ: Creative Competitions.

Moore, J., & Pachon, H. (1985). *Hispanics of the U.S.* Englewood Cliffs, NJ: Prentice-Hall.

Morgan, L. (1995, April 25). Campbell a busy man but finds time to be a friend to Athens teen. *Athens Banner-Herald, 164*(81), 1, 10.

Myers, R. E., & Torrance, E. P. (1986). *Imagining.* Mansfield Center, CT: Creative Learning Press.

Noller, R. B., & Frey, B. R. (1995). Mentoring for the continuing development of lost prizes. In McCluskey, P. A. Baker, S.C. O'Hagan, & D. J. Treffinger (Eds.), *Lost prizes* (pp. 203–212). Sarasota, FL: Center for Creative Studies.

Nugent, B. (1980, October). The corporate mentor. *Republic Scene, 2*(10), 50–57.

Osborn, A. F. (1963). *Applied imagination* (3rd ed.). New York: Scribner's.

Parker, W. M. (1988). *Consciousness-raising: A primer for multicultural counseling.* Springfield, IL: Charles C. Thomas.

Parnes, S. J. (1967). *Creative behavior guidebook.* New York: Charles Scribner's.

Pedersen, P. (1988). *A handbook for developing multicultural awareness.* Alexandria, VA: American Association for Counseling and Development.

Powell, Gen. C. L. (1997, April 27). Will you help? *Parade Magazine,* 4–6.

Presbury, J. (1986). *Icarus: To E. Paul Torrance, Christa McAuliffe, and the other great teachers-challengers of the world.* Harrisburg, VA: James Madison University.

Project XL: Inventive thinking resource directory. (1989, April). Washington, DC: U.S. Patent and Trademark Office.

Sisk, D. (1993). *Systemic training educational programs for underserved pupils (Project Step-Up).* Washington, DC: U.S. Department of Education.

Slater, J. (1977, January). Stevie Wonder: The genius of the man and his music. *Ebony,* 29–36.

Sue, D. W., & Sue, D. (1990). *Counseling the culturally different.* New York: John Wiley.

Torrance, E. P. (1970). *Encouraging creativity in the classroom.* Dubuque, IA: William C. Brown.

Torrance, E. P. (1973). What gifted disadvantaged children can teach their teachers. *Gifted Child Quarterly, 17,* 243–249.

Torrance, E. P. (1974). Interscholastic brainstorming and creative problem solving competition for the creatively gifted. *Gifted Child Quarterly, 18*, 3–7.

Torrance, E. P. (1977). *Discovery and nurturance of giftedness in the culturally different.* Reston, VA: Council for Exceptional Children.

Torrance, E. P. (1979a). An instructional model for enhancing incubation. *Journal for Creative Behavior, 13*(1), 23–35.

Torrance, E. P. (1980). Growing up creatively gifted: A 22-year longitudinal study. *Creative Child and Adult Quarterly, 5*(1), 148–158, 170.

Torrance, E. P. (1984). *Mentor relationships.* Buffalo, NY: Bearly Limited.

Torrance, E. P., Murdock, M., & Fletcher, D. (1996). *Creative problem solving through role playing.* Prætoria, RSA: Benedic Books.

Torrance, E. P., & Safter, H. T. (1990). *The incubation model of teaching.* Buffalo, NY: Bearly Limited.

Witt, G. (1968). *The life enrichment program: A brief history.* New Haven, CT: LEAP Inc. (Mimeographed).

Witt, G. (1971). The life enrichment activity program: A continuing program for creative, disadvantaged children. *Journal of Research and Development in Education, 4*(3), 67–73.

Woodkowski, R. J., & Jaynes, J. H. (1990). *Eager to learn.* San Francisco: Jossey-Bass.

Wood, K. M., & Geisman, J. L. (1989). *Families at risk.* New York: Human Sciences Press.

APPENDICIES

APPENDIX A
99 WAYS TO SAY
"VERY GOOD"

1. You're on the right track now!
2. You've got it made.
3. SUPER
4. That's RIGHT!
5. That's good.
6. You're really working hard today.
7. You are very good at that.
8. That's coming along nicely.
9. GOOD WORK!
10. That's very much better.
11. I'm happy to see you working like that.
12. Exactly right.
13. I'm proud of the way you worked today.
14. You're doing that much better today.
15. You've just about got it.
16. That's the best you've ever done.
17. You're doing a good job.
18. THAT'S IT!
19. Now you've figured it out.
20. That's quite an improvement.
21. GREAT!
22. I knew you could do it.
23. Congratulations!
24. Not bad.
25. Keep working on it. You're improving.
26. Now you have it.
27. You are learning fast.
28. Good for you!
29. Couldn't have done it better myself.
30. Aren't you proud of yourself?
31. One more time and you'll have it.

32. You really make my job fun.
33. That's the right way to do it.
34. You're getting better every day.
35. You did it that time.
36. That's not half bad.
37. Nice going.
38. You haven't missed a thing.
39. WOW!
40. That's the way.
41. Keep up the good work.
42. TERRIFIC!
43. Nothing can stop you now.
44. That's the way to do it!
45. SENSATIONAL!
46. You've got your brain in gear today.
47. That's better.
48. That was first class work.
49. EXCELLENT!
50. That's the best ever.
51. You've just about mastered it.
52. PERFECT!
53. That's better than ever!
54. Much better!
55. WONDERFUL!
56. You must have been practicing.
57. You did that very well.
58. FINE!
59. Nice going.
60. You're really going to town.
61. OUTSTANDING!
62. FANTASTIC!
63. TREMENDOUS!
64. That's how to handle that!
65. Now that's what I call a fine job.
66. That's great.
67. Right on!
68. You're really improving.

69. You're doing beautifully.
70. Superb!
71. Good remembering!
72. You've got that down pat.
73. You certainly did well today
74. Keep it up!
75. Congratulations. You got ____ right.
76. You did a lot of work today.
77. Well look at you go!
78. That's it!
79. I'm very proud of you.
80. Marvelous.
81. I like that.
82. Way to go!
83. Now you have the hang of it!
84. You're doing fine.
85. Good thinking.
86. You are really learning a lot.
87. Good going.
88. I've never seen anyone do it better.
89. Keep on trying!
90. You outdid yourself today.
91. Good for you.
92. I think you've got it now.
93. That's a good boy/girl.
94. Good job, (student's name).
95. You figured that out fast.
96. You remembered!
97. That's really nice.
98. That kind of work makes me happy.
99. It's such a pleasure to be with you when you work like that.

APPENDIX B
SUGGESTED READINGS

Blackwell, J. E. (1989). Mentoring: An action strategy for increasing minority faculty. *Academe*, 75, 8–14.

Boston, B. O. (1976). *The sorcerer's apprentice: A case study in the role of the mentor*. Reston, VA: Council for Exceptional Children.

Collins, A. (1986). The role of the mentor in the experience of change. In W. A. Gray & M. M. Gray (Eds.), *Mentoring: Aid to excellence* (pp. 94–101). Vancouver, Canada: International Association for Mentoring.

Collins, E. G. C., & Scott, P. (1978). Everyone who makes it has a mentor. *Harvard Business Revue*, 56(4), 80–101.

Diamond, H. (1978, Winter). Patterns of leadership. *Educational Horizons*, 57(2), 59–62.

Gehrke, N. (1988). Toward a definition of mentoring. *Theory into Practice*, 27(3), 190–194.

Guthrie, J. W., & Wynne, E. (1971). *New models for American Education*. Englewood Cliffs, NJ: Prentice-Hall.

Josefowitz, N. (1980). *Paths to power*. Reading, MA: Addison-Wesley.

Kanter, R. M. (1977). *Men and women of the corporation*. New York City: Basic Books.

Lengel, A. (1989). Mentee/Mentor: Someone in my corner. *Gifted Child Today*, 21(1), 27–29.

Noller, R. M. (1982). *Mentoring: A voiced scarf*. Buffalo, NY: Bearly Limited.

Noller, R. M., & Frey, B. R. (1983). *Mentoring: An annotated bibliography*. Buffalo, NY: Bearly Limited.

Redmond, S. P. (1990). Mentoring and cultural diversity in academic settings. *American Behavioral Scientists*, 34(2), 188–200.

Reilly, J. (1992). *Mentoring: The essential guide for schools and businesses*. Dayton, Ohio: Ohio Psychology Press.

Shallcross, D. J., & Sisk, D. A. (1982). *The growing person*. Englewood Cliffs, NJ: Prentice-Hall.

Sheehy, G. (1981). *Pathfinders*. New York: William Morrow.

Wickman, F. (1997). *Mentoring*. Chicago: Irwin Professional Publishing.

APPENDIX C
WHERE TO OBTAIN INFORMATION ON MENTOR MATERIALS

Bearly Limited
149 York Street
Buffalo, NY 14213

International Centre for Mentoring
Suite 500 - 1200 West Pender St.
Vancouver, B.C.
Canada V6E 2S9

Prufrock Press
Post Office Box 8813
Waco, Texas, 76714-8813

Scholastic Testing Service, Inc.
480 Meyer Road
Bensenville, IL 60106-8056

Linking Lifetimes Programs
- Birmingham, AL (205) 979-4341
- Los Angeles, CA (213) 390-6641
- Hartford, CT (203) 525-4451
- Washington, DC (202) 265-8200
- Miami, FL (305) 633-6481
- St. Petersburg, FL (813) 521-1853
- Springfield, MA (413) 737-8911
- Detroit, MI (313) 535-2970
- Syracuse, NY (315) 422-5638
- Portland, OR (503) 280-5780
- Memphis, TN (901) 577-2500

Local Chamber of Commerce and other civic organizations who sponsor mentoring programs

Big Brothers and Big Sisters

The Boys and Girls Clubs of America

100 Black Men of America

The National Council for Black Women

National Governors' Association

America's Promise—The Alliance for Youth, (888) 559-6884

National Mentoring Partnership at http://www.mentoring.org

Learn Well Mentors at http://www.learnwell.org

APPENDIX D
PROGRAMS FOR
CREATIVE DEVELOPMENT

Future Problem Solving Program

This program is the brainchild of Dr. E. Paul Torrence and Pansy Torrance who sensed a need for creatively gifted youngsters to develop richer images of the future and to expand their creativity. Students use the six steps of the creative problem solving model (Osborn, 1963; Parnes, 1967; Isaken & Treffinger, 1985) to attack and resolve predicted problems of the future (Crabbe, 1981). Participation has increased during each of its 23 years of existence and now includes a primary division. The FPS Program has grown from a state competition to an international competition and curricular program. For further information contact: Future Problem Solving Program, 2500 Packard Rd., Ann Arbor, MI, 48104-6827.

Odyssey of the Mind

This program made its debut in 1978 when Sam Micklus and Theodore Gourley believed that mental games could be played with the same enthusiasm and competitive spirit as physical games (Micklus, 1988). They further believed that the mind could be trained through practice and exercise to reach its fullest potential. The program provides structured creative problem solving opportunities as well as opportunities for fluency and flexibility of thinking. This program has also grown since its inception and has become an international program as well. For further information contact: Odyssey of the Mind Association Inc., P.O. Box 27, Glassboro, NJ 08028.

Invent America

A relatively new program (Project XL, 1989), Invent America has been developed by the U.S. Patent Model Foundation and is designed to help children learn to develop their creativity, ingenuity, and motivation. Students participate by creating inventive solutions to problem needs in school, in the community, or at home with parent and teacher support. The competition begins at the local school level and culminates with the winners being presented patents in Washington, DC. For more information contact: U.S. Patent Model Foundation, 1331 Pennsylvania Ave., Suite 903, Washington, DC 20004.

Young Game Inventors Contest

Children who are not more than 13 years old and who like to play and invent games will find the *Young Game Inventors Contest* of great interest. The purpose is to provide young students an opportunity to apply their creativity by inventing a board game. Entries are judged for fun and creative ideas. The grand prize winner receives a four-night, expenses-paid trip for three to San Francisco, the chance to have the game manufactured by University Games, and much more. For detailed information, contact Young Game Inventors Contest, *U.S. Kids*, P.O. Box 567, Indianapolis, IN 46206.

Young American Patriotic Art Award

Through the Young American Creative Patriotic Art Awards, high school students express their artistic talents and demonstrate their patriotism while becoming eligible for funds to further their art education. Students may use watercolor, pencil, pastel, charcoal, tempera, crayon, acrylic, pen and ink, or oil on paper or canvas in their entries. These are judged on originality of concept, patriotism expressed, content and clarity of ideas, design, use of color, technique, and total impact or execution and contrast. Awards include:

$3,000 first prize; $2,000 second prize; $1,500 third prize; $1,000 fourth prize; and $500 fifth prize. The first prize also includes an expenses-paid weekend to the American Academy of Achievement and an expenses-paid trip to be honored at the next Veterans of Foreign Wars Auxiliary National Convention. For more information write Ladies Auxiliary to the Veterans of Foreign Wars, 406 W. 34th St., Kansas City, MO 64111.

National Teen Business Plan Competition

To give teens an opportunity to increase their understanding of the concepts, tools, and responsibilities of business ownership while putting their own entrepreneurial dreams on paper, the *National Teen Business Plan Competition* was established. Boys and girls who are 13 to 19 years old may apply. Entries are judged on the quality of the business plan. Five female and five male winners receive a trip to a major U.S. city for the next national competition. The winners also receive a resource kit of products and services. Furthermore, they are matched with business owners who act as business coaches by providing additional support and follow-up to the youngsters' exploration of business and entrepreneurship. For more information, contact: *National Teen Business Plan Competition*, An Income of Her Own, P.O. Box 987, Santa Barbara, CA 93102.

The Kids' Hall of Fame

Students who have made or are making a positive difference for themselves, their family, school, community, state, country, or world should know about *The Kids' Hall of Fame*. Students must be 14 years old or younger. Five national grand prize winners will each receive a $10,000 post-high school educational scholarship and a trip to Washington, DC, for themselves and two parents or guardians. Twenty-five first prize winners each receive a $100 U.S. Savings Bond. For more information, contact *The Kids' Hall of Fame* by Pizza Hut, P.O. Box 92477, Libertyville, IL 60092.

Guidepost Young Writers Contest

For those writers in your school, the *Guideposts Young Writers Contest* was developed to promote young people's writing talent and their awareness of how faith plays a part in their everyday lives. High school juniors and seniors or homeschooled students equivalent to these grades may enter. The first prize winner receives a $6,000 scholarship; second prize, a $5,000 scholarship; third prize, a $4,000 scholarship, and fourth through eighth prizes, $1,000 scholarships each. The ninth through 25th prize winners receive a portable electronic typewriter. Scholarships are designated for the colleges or schools of the winners' choice. To get information, write *Guideposts Young Writers Contest, Guideposts Magazine*, 16 E. 34th St., New York, NY 10016.

NOTE: We are indebted to Drs. Frances Karnes and Tracy Riley for the last five of the above activities. "Competitions: Developing and nurturing talents." *Gifted Child Today Magazine, 19*(2), 14-15, 49.

APPENDIX E
EXAMPLES AND INCIDENTS
IN MENTORING IN THE
CULTURE OF POVERTY

Mentoring One on Two
by Neil Satterfield

Martin and Kersey

Martin and Kersey are two African American boys in the fourth grade in a Metro Atlanta Elementary School. I was put in touch with them through The Atlanta Project. Martin was from a single-parent family with limited education. He had moved five times in the last three years, each time changing school districts. In my experience as a mentor and through programs working with poor children, this constant moving is a major detriment to a youth's progress academically. Principals and counselors tell me that they believe the dropout rate among those constantly moved is triple that of those who remain in the same residence two or more years at a time. Martin is a reasonably smart child who, according to his teacher, is very easily distracted, begins work without listening to instructions, and presents behavioral problems that disrupt the class. She felt that he would benefit from one-on-one attention, especially from a man. His need for attention became evident through his eagerness for our mentoring sessions. The teacher said he was beginning to anticipate my visits so much that if I came even a few minutes late he began to show anxiety or concern.

Kersey lived with his mother and step-father. His mother was rather strict and very protective. She was somewhat suspicious of anyone who would volunteer his time to mentor young children. As it turned out, she was a supervisor in a correctional institution and had encountered a few child molesters among the prison population. Kersey was also bright but apparently unmotivated to address

107

his seat work in class. He seldom did his homework when assigned and was perceived by his teacher as impetuous.

Neither of these young men knew how to set goals or plan before acting. I tried several activities to get them to read directions before launching into a task. I tried the age old trick of presenting them with an activity which ended with: "If you have read all of the directions then write your name at the top of the page and do *nothing more*." Did they fail to read all of the instructions before acting. Yes!

One day, out of frustration, I decided to try a more physically active learning challenge which required planning before acting if one was to succeed. We usually were given the Art Room for our mentoring sessions. It was seldom occupied, and it had numerous chairs and tables in it. On this day, I had brought two Snickers™ bars as incentive/reward if they succeeded. We set up what amounted to a maze and the Snickers™ bar was always placed at the destination. Through practice runs we established what was a reasonable time to reach the destination—something like 12 to 15 seconds. Then came the surprise. They would be rewarded only if they could complete the maze *blindfolded*! They each tried it once blindfolded unsuccessfully. After the usual charges of "Not fair," I told them it was really something they could accomplish if they planned ahead. They were permitted to study the maze which I changed each time, but they had to then put on the blindfold to actually do it. The first couple of tries were unsuccessful. Kersey came close so he was convinced he could do it.

Martin was more apprehensive. Kersey succeeded on his third try. Martin did not and began to sulk a little. When Kersey got the first Snickers™ it was tough for Martin to take, mainly because Kersey usually had the edge in their academic competition. I discouraged competition and generated learning games that usually required them to work as a team to succeed. But I couldn't deny that for these two competition was a good motivator. We had a little object lesson on not sulking and complaining because it seldom helped solve a problem.

At this point, I looked Martin in the eye and told him that if he would just concentrate and plan his attack, I was sure he'd make it.

He studied the course. Then he wanted to know if any route to the Snickers™ was acceptable. I said yes but reminded him that he may not move the furniture. We put the blindfold on. Martin immediately went to his hands and knees and crawled under two tables and around one chair. It was the most direct route possible. He then stood up and felt around on the table before him. He got the Snickers™ bar in about six seconds! Martin was one happy and proud kid! While Martin never voiced this, it was pretty apparent that he relished the fact that he did it in much less time than Kersey.

When we debriefed by discussing the value of planning a strategy before executing the task, I then asked them to quickly tell me how it would be helpful in class. They named 11 bona fide and useful examples. Then the bell rang and it was time for them to return to their classes. They promised not to eat the candy in class or on the school bus going home. Each of their teachers reported that the boys were much better about following directions. It was a good day.

Dropouts
by Neil Satterfield

In working with inner city teens, mostly Black males, it became evident that school attendance and performance were poor. Only 20 percent of the 30 or so youth we worked with were doing passing work or better in all subjects. Three of them had better than a "C" average. It was, likewise, abundantly clear that most of them had the potential to make passing grades and finish high school. There were myriad reasons which we've all heard, such as boredom, too difficult, teacher dislike or perceived dislike of them by teachers, no fun, rather stay home or play basketball, and so forth. Despite the fact that these youth live in one of the most violent areas in Atlanta, only a few even mentioned fear of violence. The intervening strategies had to meet certain criteria to be effective: (a) must be realistic, (b) must *not* be overwhelming, (c) must have built in successes, and (d) must be able to motivate them.

I started with five Black teenage males—one 15, two 16, and a pair of twins who were recently 18 and had dropped out of school.

Essentially, they dropped out because they were too far behind and, therefore, much older than most of their classmates, which was embarrassing. They also admitted that they lacked certain fundamentals to understand some of the "new stuff." None of the five had a system of study that worked for them. While some teachers may quarrel with my approach (certainly some of their teachers), so far it has worked for them.

Starting with several typical texts, I asked how they would go about studying if they were assigned Chapters 3 and 4 to know for a test at the end of the week. "Just start reading," said two. "Pay attention to the paragraph headings and bold print," suggested another. I commended that idea. Only one said anything about the Chapter Review, and that was sort of a guess as he read my face which must have signaled "What else?" My advice was to never just start reading the chapter unless it's a novel or something for fun. We then talked about Table of Contents, Index, Glossaries, and most importantly, Chapter Summaries.

"So, do you want to save time, do well on tests, retain the important stuff?" I asked. That plus the idea of "shocking the teacher" with new academic prowess, and "beating the system" with these new "tricks" in learning all had appeal, and I had five guys grinning like this might be fun. As an aside, several of these young men had teachers who checked their notebooks to see if they had "complete notes," whatever that means. Okay, while I generally found my college students who constantly took notes (and whose faces I seldom saw) to be only average students, I realized that students have to play the game of satisfying the teacher even when their approach or class rules were, in my opinion, limiting learning. This issue arose when I was teaching the guys how to "psyche the teacher." It was a matter of listening carefully for what the teacher seemed to emphasize by change in inflection or writing on the board. Likewise, I suggested that they be aware when a teacher repeated a concept, in the *lecture* (which by the way is often overused to the neglect of group interaction and "hands-on" experiments). If they did repeat, make a note of the concept or main idea. I specifically encouraged taking notes in a brief manner such as "key phrase," single word, or concept. It would work even for the teachers who checked notebooks for complete notes, since as students, they could go home and elaborate on the ideas the teacher espoused in his or her lecture. Homework and notebook checks never took place until the next day and usually at the end of the week, which coincidentally were high absentee days.

These youth have initiated this "system" and, so far, have improved their grades significantly. The twins have enrolled in a GED course and meet with me on Wednesday nights for support or assistance. The three of this group who are still in school no longer tell their parents that they have no homework. They actually do it, using this new, shorter method. Whatever they do, it is more than they were doing! Keeping them motivated and not distracted seems to be the major challenge now.

Challenging these young men in new and different ways so they realize the importance of learning is critical. It has to be illustrated in everyday life why math, language, and science are important. They need to know the relevance to real life and to recognize that social skills and academic skills can make a difference in how people perceive them and even whether or not they can get a decent job. Learning how to apply percentages is how they can determine whether or not a basketball player or a baseball player had a good night. It was easy to teach them percentages, which few retained from school, by specifying that they should divide the "big number" into the "little number" by illustrating that a baseball player's batting average is derived by dividing the number of "at bats" into the number of "hits." And in basketball, shooting percentage was found by dividing "Attempted Goals" into "Goals Made." From there we could transfer that knowledge into business, that is customers engaged versus sales made, and so forth. Keeping score in bowling was another method of teaching cumulative scoring and averages.

On a couple of occasions, I enticed some analytical thinking by taking three Frisbees™ onto a ball field and inquired as to how we could predict the distance they would each fly. Which would go further? Would the diameter of the Frisbees™ (we relearned diameter and circumference) be a good predictor? Lots of speculation took place. Then we tried them out. We raised more questions than answers.

Variables came up by the truckload! Who throws them, how hard, how well, into the wind, with the wind, and so forth. Then the questions of whether or not there would be a linear relationship between the size of the Frisbees and the distance they traveled. After much discussion and trial throws, it was recognized that the aerodynamics of the tiny Frisbee™ must be a factor (it fluttered and died at a disproportionate short distance). Yet the middle size and large Frisbee™ did seem to travel distances very close to the relative size of the two.

The bottom line—the "system" has given up on too many economically disadvantaged youth. The dearth of books, magazines, or intellectually challenging experiences accounts for an awful lot of their failures. Add to that, parents, guardians, and school systems that expect too little and make little effort to make learning innovative and fun and you have the perfect formula for unproductive citizens. Racism, sexism, and violence remain in the social structure and behavioral results perpetuate all of these negatives.

Here are some other activities I have introduced to these teens, in a few instances to the point where some of them were saying "Hey Doc, we've done this before." That's a clue that we should switch to something else, or better yet, to ask them how else they could learn the objective we were teaching. Anyhow, here is a short list with a brief explanation of how each is played: (Needless to say, one may vary these endlessly.)

1. Have a map puzzle (best made of wood) and have teams of three or four people take turns, one person at a time, depending upon the age and ability level and ask them to remove from the puzzle certain states or countries, return to their team, and name the capitol of each.

2. Memory Games—while this is admittedly a lower order of learning on most hierarchies, things like times tables, geography, names of authors, books, and historic events are learned by memory. Challenging the students to come up with "hooks" (prompts or cues) can enhance memory skills. Sometimes at the end of a given exercise, it is useful to make them all dispose of whatever they have written and see, as a group, what they have retained. It's always better than at the start, so everybody wins!

3. We've put on "Keen Teen" contests which were a broad measure of academic skills. They included math, science, social studies, language, and creative problem solving exercises. These tournaments usually mixed in some athletic skills such as basketball free throws, pool shooting, and ping pong. Those were used as a means of making the tournament not seem too much like tests at school.

4. I introduced a vocabulary game which was made like the pieces in a board game. We turned our teen room into a "race track" with grids crossing the track to represent the spaces they could move up when they got the right answer. One space advancement for a correct spelling, another for an adequate definition or synonym, and a third space for putting the word into a proper sentence correctly. I learned from experience that this exercise "drags" if it goes on too long. So make the race short, a sprint, if you will. Three or four players in a 10 to 12 link race is plenty.

5. Another interesting word game is to take the letter blocks of a Scrabble™ game and distribute them equally among three or four groups. Be sure the point count of the blocks is equal and the number of blocks is equal (this takes a little preparation). Then have the groups, in a limited time, make a sensible sentence using as many blocks, or more importantly point count, as possible. Blocks not used count against the score compiled.

We also provided lunch, usually pizza with fruit, drinks, and dessert. That helped get good attendance and made it more fun. We also sneaked in a personal interview to learn more about the family lives of these young people, as well as what they dreamed about, liked the most, and feared the most. And ... no small factor, were the awards of trophies for the best in each event.

* Needless to say, some of the better board games are fun and useful. Boggle™, Scrabble™, Checkers and Chess, short form Monopoly™, and one I introduced which I doubt is original but may be, is Dictionary. This is played mainly with players who are performing at the middle school level or higher. It is best played with five to eight players. Each player, in turn, gets to find a word in the dictionary that he or she believes the other players will not know. The "dealer" (person with the dictionary) then reads the word aloud, spells it, and asks for a definition from the players each of whom has pencil and paper on which to write his or her own creative definition. If, however, a player knows or thinks he or she knows the *real definition* of the word, then the player writes it down in his own words. If one does not know the word then he or she writes a definition he or she believes he can get other players to vote for as the real one. The game is often hilarious, and it teaches people new words and definitions which by the way are reinforced by repeating all the words used with their real definitions at the end of the game. Scoring is done thusly:

1) A point is given to the "dealer" for every wrong definition from the group. This is usually the best time for the player to score.

2) A point is also given to any player for every player who wrongly votes for his or her phony definition.

3) A point is given to any player who defined the dealer's word correctly.

To avoid unnecessary contention, it is recommended that the dictionary version be read and then the version of the player. It is not necessary that the player's definition be exact or as long—just that the meaning is essentially the same. The player group usually votes "Up" or "Down" on whether or not the players' definition is close enough. If there is reason to believe this may become too argumentative, an adult referee can be appointed to make the decision.

ABOUT THE AUTHORS

E. Paul Torrance

E. Paul Torrance, now retired, is the former Alumni Foundation Distinguished Professor of Educational Psychology at the University of Georgia. He has had extensive experience as a high school teacher and counselor, a university teacher and counselor, counselor of disabled veterans, counselor of veterans receiving dishonorable discharges, teacher of courses on the learning problems of economically disadvantaged children, and a mentor of disadvantaged young people. His longitudinal research has raised concerns about the lack of mentoring of economically disadvantaged children and youth. He is the author of *Mentor Relationships: How They Aid Creative Achievement, Endure, Change, and Die.*

Kathy Goff

Kathy Goff co-authored with E. Paul Torrance *Mentor's Guide and Protégé's Handbook*. She has extensive experience as a high school and college teacher and researcher. She is now the technical assistant and outreach coordinator of the University Affiliated Program at the University of Oklahoma Health Sciences Center. She holds adjunct faculty appointments in the occupational and the physical therapy departments in the College of Allied Health and in the department of pediatrics in the College of Medicine at the University of Oklahoma Health Sciences Center and in the department of family and child relations in the College of Human Environmental Sciences at Oklahoma State University. Dr. Goff has conducted pioneering research in the areas of creativity, disabilities, and gerontology.

Neil B. Satterfield

Dr. Satterfield, now retired, is a former professor and head of the social work department of Armstrong College and Savannah State College. He has had extensive experience as a social worker, and college teacher of social work, and has experience in working with economically disadvantaged children and families, teaching economically disadvantaged children, and mentoring them both in one-on-one and small group relationships. At the present, he and his wife are volunteer workers in a variety of community agencies working with economically disadvantaged children and their families. He has become qualified as a domestic and divorce mediator, pioneering in this new field where mediation is required in all divorce cases.

SUBJECT INDEX

NAME INDEX

A
Adams, A., 79
Adams, J. Q., 79
Allen-Hagen, B., 13, 66
Atkinson, D. R., 9

B
Blackwell, J. E., 99
Boston, B. O., 99
Bova, V. M., 48

C
Campbell, C., 7
Close, J. J., 13
Collins, A., 99
Collins, E. G. C., 99
Collins, N. W., 48
Cox, B., 7
Crabbe, A., 103

E
Edison, T., 79
Ehrlich, V., 85

F
Fletcher, D., 45
Frey, B. R., iv, 99

G
Gehrke, N., 99
Geisman, J. L., 66
Goff, K., 115
Gordy, Jr., B., 80
Gourley, T., 103
Guthrie, J. W., 99

I
Isaksen, S. G., 71, 103

THIS COPY IS THE
MOST RECENT
EDITION OF TITLE.

DATE CHECKED:

1. 2008.6.13

2. _____

3. _____

4. _____

5. _____

NEW EDITION FOUND ☐

DATE:

EDITION # _____

PUB. YR. _____

RECOMMENDED TITLE:

_____